W0185158

Collaborate

A1+ – A2

Claire Thacker

STUDENT'S BOOK 1

CAMBRIDGE
UNIVERSITY PRESS

CONTENTS

STARTER

WELCOME!

VOCABULARY

Months

S.01 **1** **Write the months in the correct order. Listen, check and repeat.**

April	August	December	February
January	June	July	March	May
November	October	September	

January

Get it right!

In English, months and days of the week start with a capital letter. Is it the same in your language?

2 **Complete the sentences. Compare with a partner.**

1 This month is … .

2 My birthday is in … .

Cardinal and ordinal numbers

3 **Write the numbers.**

1 The number of letters in my name.

2 The date today.

3 The number of people in my house.

4 **Find the correct number.**

1 Start with 10.
Add 3.
Subtract 2.
What's your number?
What's the ordinal number?

2 Start with 25.
Subtract 6.
Add 12.
What's your number?
What's the ordinal number?

LEARN TO LEARN

Learning numbers together

Learn and practise cardinal and ordinal numbers together.

23 – twenty-three, 23rd – twenty-third

S.02 **5** **Listen. Write the numbers you hear.**

1 a 17 b (70)   3 a 12th b 20th

2 a 13 b 30   4 a 51st b 61st

6 **Use it!** **Take turns to say a cardinal number. Your partner says the ordinal number.**

S.03 **7** **Listen and complete the sentences with the date.**

1 Laura's birthday is on *24th July*.

2 Onur's birthday is on … .

3 Bella's birthday is on … .

4 Nico's birthday is on … .

8 **Complete the sentences. Then tell your partner.**

1 My birthday is on … .

2 Today is … .

Colours

S.04 **9** **Add the colours and write the new colour. Listen, check and repeat.**

1 *red + blue = purple*

S.05 **10** **Do the quiz with a partner. Listen and check.**

THE GREAT BIG NUMBER QUIZ!!

1 The number of countries in the world is … .
a 195 b 100 c 95

2 … million people speak English as their first language.
a 3 b 36 c 360

3 There are … seconds in a year.
a 36,536,000 b 31,536,000 c 35,636,000

4 … million people have the same birthday as you.
a 19 b 6 c 10

READING

An online profile

1 **Look at the photos. Where do you think Diana and Thiago are from? Read the profiles quickly and check your answers.**

S.06 **2** **Read the profiles again and listen. Are the sentences *T* (true) or *F* (false)?**

1. Diana is from Granada. T
2. Miranda is Turkish.
3. Diana's favourite place is her bedroom.
4. Thiago is from São Paulo.
5. Thiago's favourite colour is blue.
6. Thiago is good at football.

3 **Find nationalities in the profiles to match the countries.**

1. Spain Spanish
2. Mexico
3. Turkey
4. Brazil
5. the USA

4 **Copy and complete the table with the countries and nationalities. Can you add any more?**

Country	Nationality
Australia	[1] Australian
[2]	Canadian
China	[3]
[4]	German
Poland	[5]
the UK	[6]

WELCOME TO MY LIFE!

Home | Profile | Photos | Events

Hi! My name's Diana. I'm from Granada in Spain. I'm 13 years old.

In this photo, I'm with Miranda and Suki. They're my best friends. They aren't Spanish. Miranda's Mexican and Suki's Turkish.

My birthday is on 9th March. When is your birthday?

My favourite colour is blue.

My favourite place is my bedroom. Guess what colour it is!

My dream is to be a singer like Rihanna. She's brilliant! 🙂 Are you a good singer?

What's your name? How old are you? Let me know! 🙂

Hello! My name's Thiago. I'm from Brasília. It's the capital of Brazil. I'm Brazilian. I'm 14. I'm with Bruno and Victor in this photo. They're my best friends. We're at the same American school, but I'm not in their class.

My favourite colours are yellow and green. Can you guess why?

My favourite number is 10.

My dream is to be a footballer like Neymar Júnior. He's amazing! I'm good, too! 🙂 Are you a football fan?

What's your name? Where are you from? Write soon!

5 **Voice it!** **Complete the sentences with your ideas. Compare with a partner.**

1. Diana's bedroom is … because … .
2. Thiago's favourite colours are yellow and green because … .
3. Thiago's dream is to be like Neymar because … .

GRAMMAR IN ACTION

Subject pronouns and possessive adjectives

Watch video S.1
Where is Isabella from?
What is Martin's dream?

Subject pronouns	Possessive adjectives	Subject pronouns	Possessive adjectives
I	**my**	It	**its**
You	**your**	We	**our**
He	**his**	They	**their**
She	**her**		

Grammar reference p126

1 Choose the correct words.

1 Alana is (*my*) / *I* best friend.
2 *Our* / *We* aren't from Brazil. *Our* / *We* 're from Spain.
3 *Her* / *She* name is Luna. *Her* / *She* 's 13.
4 *Their* / *They* names are Kit and Bella. *Their* / *They* aren't British.

Verb *be*

Affirmative	I**'m** (**am**) from Granada. She**'s** (**is**) brilliant! He**'s** (**is**) amazing! We**'re** (**are**) at the same American school. They**'re** (**are**) my best friends.
Negative	They **aren't** Spanish. Miranda **isn't** Turkish. I**'m not** in their class.
Questions and short answers	How old **are** you? **Are** you a football fan? Yes, I **am**. / No, I'm **not**. **Is** Thiago 12? Yes, he **is**. / No, he **isn't**. **Are** Bruno and Victor Brazilian? Yes, they **are**. / No, they **aren't**.

Grammar reference p124

S.07 **2** Complete the profile with the correct form of *be*. Guess the person. Listen and check.

His birthday [1]is (✓) on 1st March.
He [2]… (✗) American. He [3]… (✓) Canadian.
My favourite songs [4]… (✓) *Boyfriend* and *Sorry*.
[5]… (?) he your favourite singer?

3 Write questions with the verb *be*.

1 you / 12? *Are you 12?*
2 you / from / Ankara?
3 your best friends / in your class?
4 your teacher / English?
5 orange / your favourite colour?
6 today / 19th June?

4 **Use it!** Ask and answer the questions in Exercise 3.

Question words

5 Match the question words with their functions.

1 What — d
2 Where
3 When
4 How old
5 Who

a age
b people
c places
d things
e time and dates

Grammar reference p126

6 Complete the questions with *is* or *are*.

1 Where *are* you from?
2 How old … you?
3 When … your birthday?
4 Who … your best friend?
5 What … your favourite colour?

7 **Use it!** Ask and answer the questions in Exercise 6.

VOCABULARY AND LISTENING

Classroom objects

S.08 **1** **Match the words in the box with the picture. Listen, check and repeat.**

~~board~~ calculator chair dictionary door notebook pen pencil poster ruler table window

1 *board*

LEARN TO LEARN

Organising your notebook

It's important to organise your vocabulary notebook at the start of term. Divide the pages to record new vocabulary. Write a translation and draw a picture to help you remember the words.

Classroom objects	Translation	Picture

2 **Organise your notebook and write new vocabulary from this unit.**

3 COLLABORATE **Test a partner. Take turns to say a word in your language. Your partner says it in English. Can you remember all the new words?**

A talk

S.09 **4** **Listen and choose the correct answer.**

Stefan is …

a a teacher. b a student.

S.09 **5** **Listen again. Choose the correct answer.**

1 Stefan is in Year *7 / 10*.
2 Stefan *is / isn't* a friendly person.
3 It's the students' *first / second* day at the school.
4 At the end, Luiza *is / isn't* in the classroom.

6 Use it! **Answer the questions with a partner.**

1 What classroom objects are on your table?
2 What is in your bag?

GRAMMAR IN ACTION

Whose + possessive pronouns

Watch video S.2
What classroom objects are there?
What colour is Mia´s pen?

Whose … ?	Possessive pronouns
Whose dictionary is this?	It's **mine**.
	It's **yours**.
	It's **his**.
	It's **hers**.
	It's **ours**.
	It's **theirs**.

this, that, these, those	
 **This** is my pencil.	 **That** is my calculator.
 **These** are my notebooks.	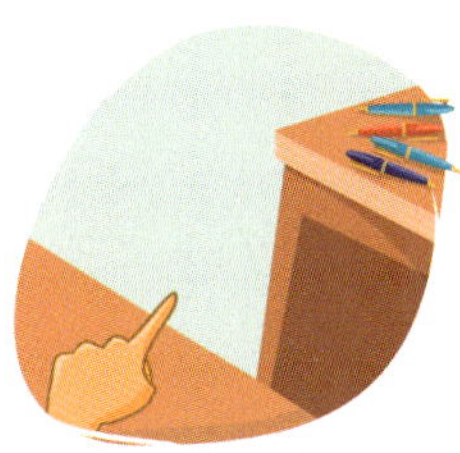 **Those** are my pens.

Grammar reference p126

1 **Complete the second sentence with a possessive pronoun.**

1 It's your pencil. It's *yours*.
2 That's his notebook. That's … .
3 This table is my table. This table is … .
4 Those are our chairs. Those are … .
5 Is this your calculator? Is this … ?
6 Are these her pens? Are these … ?

S.10 **2** **Write the questions. Then listen and match the questions with the answers.**

1 book / whose / this / is
Whose book is this? b
2 posters / those / are / whose
3 are / pens / whose / these
4 that / ruler / whose / is

a It's his.
b It's mine.
c They're hers.
d They're ours.

Imperatives

Affirmative	Negative
Close the door!	Don't be late!

Grammar reference p126

3 **Look at the grammar table. Which sentence is positive (✓)?**

S.11 **4** **Complete the instructions with the verbs in the box. Listen and check.**

don't forget ~~don't write~~ listen to use write

1 *Don't write* on the desks!
2 … new words in your notebook!
3 … to bring your pen!
4 … your teacher!
5 … a dictionary!

S.12 **5** **Listen and follow the instructions.**

6 **Use it!** **Take turns to give your partner instructions. Use classroom objects or your own ideas.**

WRITING
An informal letter

1 Read Gloria's letter. Who is Mrs Weston?

29 Upper Road
Wilmslow
Cheshire
SK52 0TY

16th September

Dear Mrs Weston,

My name is Gloria Rodriguez **and** I'm 13. I'm from Ottowa in Canada. I'm Canadian.

I'm a student at the International School. It's my first day in this school. I'm happy! I'm in class 7A. That's your class!

The students here are from all over the world. My best friends are Marco **and** Leona. They're in my class. They aren't Canadian like me. Marco is Italian **and** Leona is German.

My favourite colour is pink **and** my favourite place is my English classroom. My dream is to be a teacher – just like you!

Best wishes,

Gloria

2 Read Gloria's letter again. Which information isn't in the letter?

name age birthday country nationality names of her best friends favourite colour and place dream

3 Look at the *Useful language* box and complete the information with words from Gloria's letter.

Useful language

to start: [1]… + *Mr* (man) or *Mrs*/*Miss* (woman) + person's surname,
to end: *All the best,* or [2]…
to join two ideas in one sentence: [3]…

4 Join the sentences with *and*.

1 My name is Hugo. I'm 13 years old.
2 I'm Japanese. I'm from Tokyo.
3 My favourite number is 15. My favourite colour is red.

TASK
Write an informal letter

PLAN

5 Plan an informal letter to your teacher. Write four paragraphs. Include the following information:

your name your age
your nationality
information about your school
your best friends
your favourite colour and place
your dream

WRITE

6 Write your letter.

CHECKLIST **Remember to include:**
- the information from Exercise 5
- the address
- the date
- *Dear* + person's name at the start
- *Best wishes* or *All the best* at the end
- your name in handwriting at the end
- *and* to join ideas.

CHECK

7 COLLABORATE **Swap your letter with a partner. Has it got the items in the** CHECKLIST? How old is your friend?

1 FRIENDS AND FAMILY

LEARNING OUTCOMES

I can …

- understand texts about families and a festival
- phone a friend
- write an email
- understand how to use *have got*; possessive *'s*; questions with *How many …?*
- talk about families and describe people
- draw pictures to remember words and increase my vocabulary
- make a poster.

WATCH VIDEO 1.1

- Before you watch, are friends family?
- Watch and check. Where are Laura and Andrés from?
- Which is your favourite family? Why?

KICK-OFF! 1.1

p13

GRAMMAR IN ACTION 1.2

p15

GRAMMAR IN ACTION 1.3

p16

EVERYDAY ENGLISH 1.4

p18

GLOBETROTTERS 1.5

VOCABULARY

Family members

1.01 **1** Look at Beth's family tree. Match the names with eight other words from the box. Then listen and check.

aunt brother cousin dad daughter ~~grandad~~ granddaughter grandma grandson husband mum nephew niece sister son uncle wife

a *grandad*

1.02 **2** Look at Beth's family tree. Complete the answers with words from Exercise 1. Then listen, check and repeat.

1 Andy + Sara = husband and *wife*

2 Lizzie + Olga = mum and …

3 Amanda + Theo = grandma and …

4 Ryan + Beth = … and …

5 Lizzie + Theo = … and …

6 Victor + Andy = … and …

7 Victor + Marina = … and …

8 Theo + Beth = … and …

3 Copy and complete the diagram with the family words from Exercise 1.

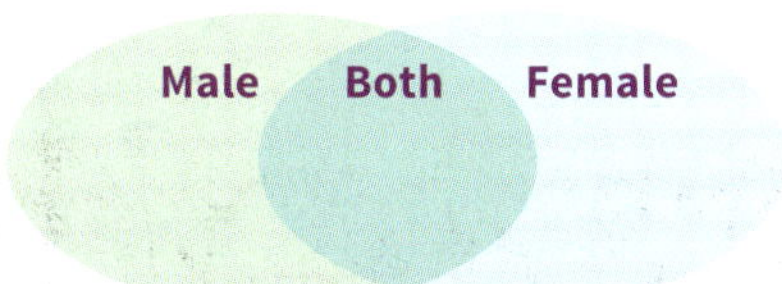

LEARN TO LEARN

Making connections

Think of examples from your own life to make connections and remember new words.

4 Draw your family tree. Use Beth's design to help you.

5 COLLABORATE Don't show your family tree. Take turns to say the name of a person in your family. Can your partner guess their relationship to you?

Carlos. *Is he your brother?* *No, he isn't. Try again.*

6 Use it! Imagine you are a famous person. Tell your partner about your family. Can your partner guess who you are?

I'm British. My brother is Harry. My wife is Kate. My children are George, Charlotte and Louis.

Are you Prince William?

Yes, I am.

Explore it!

Guess the correct answer.

A Canadian woman, Vera Sommerfeld, is a great-great-great grandma. There are … generations of women in her family.

a two b four c six

Find an interesting family fact. Then write a question for your partner to answer.

READING

A webpage

1 Tell your partner two things you know about the circus and two things you want to know about the topic.

1.03 2 Read and listen to the webpage. What is it about?

1 Typical family life
2 Life in a circus family
3 A circus school

3 Find words in the webpage to match the photos.

a

b

c

d

4 Read the webpage again. Find the correct names.

Who …

1 are trapeze artists?
2 is an acrobat and a trapeze artist?
3 is a circus teacher?
4 aren't circus performers?

5 Correct the sentences.

1 Ysabella Cortes is from a typical family.
Ysabella Cortes isn't from a typical family. She's from a circus family.
2 Robinson and Alida are brother and sister.
3 Lucas and Tomas are cousins.
4 Alida and Aurelia are friends.
5 Tino isn't old.

6 **Voice it!** Discuss the questions.

1 What is a typical family?
2 Is family life in the circus like your family life? Why / Why not?
3 What are the good and bad things about life in the circus?

Meet the Flying Cortes Family

Ysabella Wallenda-Cortes isn't from a typical family. She's from a circus family. Ysabella is a trapeze artist like her parents. Her parents' names are Robinson and Alida. She's got two brothers, Lucas and Tomas, but she hasn't got any sisters.

Ysabella's uncle and aunt are in the circus, too. Her uncle Alex is her dad's brother and he's an acrobat and a trapeze artist. Her aunt Aurelia is her mum's sister and she's one of Ysabella's teachers. Her grandparents, Olinka and Tino, are also part of the circus. Olinka isn't a performer any more. Her job is to help the rest of the family. Tino is in his 60s but he's still a tightrope walker. Lucas and Tomas haven't got jobs in the circus … yet!

Where is home? They've got two homes – one in the USA and a mobile home. The mobile home is also a school during tours. Imagine a school on wheels!

Finished? p21

Watch video 1.2
True or false?
Tess has got two brothers.
Marco has got a big family.

GRAMMAR IN ACTION

Have got: affirmative and negative

	I/You/We/They	*He/She/It*
+	They **have** (**'ve**) **got** two homes.	Ysabella **has** (**'s**) **got** two brothers.
–	Lucas and Tomas **have not** (**haven't**) **got** jobs in the circus.	She **has not** (**hasn't**) **got** any sisters.

Grammar reference p124

1 Choose the correct form of *have got*. Then check your answers in the webpage on page 12.

1. Robinson *has got* / *hasn't got* a sister in the circus.
2. Alida *has got* / *hasn't got* a sister in the circus.
3. Olinka and Tino *have got* / *haven't got* any grandsons in the circus.
4. Ysabella *has got* / *hasn't got* an aunt and an uncle in the circus.

1.04 **2** Complete the text with the correct form of *have got*. Then listen and check.

Meet this week's circus stars ...

Bibi and Bichu Tesfamariam are brothers and they're from Ethiopia. They [1]haven't got (–) any sisters.

Ethiopia [2]... (–) a circus tradition but Bibi and Bichu are brilliant jugglers. They [3]... (+) a circus school in Ethiopia. It [4]... (+) 150 students. They [5]... (+) their own circus too, called Circus Abyssinia, with some amazing Ethiopian acrobats. We think Bibi and Bichu [6]... (+) a great future!

3 Remember the information from the text in Exercise 2. Write three sentences with *have(n't)* / *has(n't) got*.

Bibi has got a brother.

4 COLLABORATE Swap sentences with your partner. Check them. Are they correct?

Possessive *'s*

Alex is her dad**'s** brother.	Her parents**'** names are Robinson and Alida.

Grammar reference p126

5 Complete the sentences. Use the words in brackets with *'s* or *s'*.

1. Aurelia's niece is Ysabella. (Aurelia)
2. Alida is ... wife. (Robinson)
3. ... names are Ysabella, Alex, Robinson and Alida. (the trapeze artists)
4. ... grandparents are Olinka and Tino. (Ysabella)
5. Aurelia is ... sister. (Alida)

6 Use it! Write true and false sentences with *'s* or *s'* and *have got*. Use the ideas below or your own ideas. Can your partner guess the false sentences?

My ...'s name ...

My ...s' house ...

My sister's classroom ... got ...

I haven't got ...

My grandparents' house is pink. They've got a big garden.

Finished? p21

VOCABULARY AND LISTENING

Describing people

1.05 **1** Put the words in the correct place in the circles. Listen, check and repeat.

beard   blonde   brown (x2)   freckles
glasses   grey (x2)   long   moustache
red   short (x2)   tall   wavy

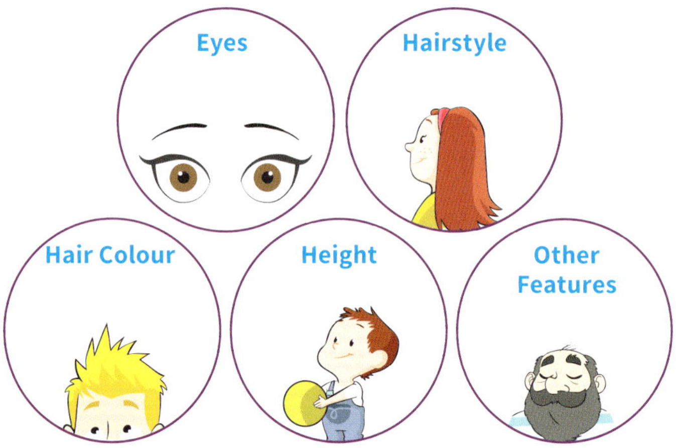

LEARN TO LEARN

Drawing pictures

Drawing pictures can help you to visualise new words and remember them more easily.

2 Draw pictures of the words in Exercise 1 in your notebook.

Describing people	Translation	Picture
brown eyes		

3 COLLABORATE Cover the words and show your pictures to a partner. Can they guess the correct words?

Get it right!

Adjectives go before nouns in English.

brown eyes **NOT** ~~*eyes brown*~~

4 Describe the people. Use words from Exercise 1.

5 Use it! Work in pairs. Take turns to describe your classmates. Can your partner guess?

He's tall. He's got short brown hair.

Is it Serge?

Yes, it is. / No, it isn't.

A conversation

1.06 **6** Look at the photo and listen. Who is the actor?

1.06 **7** Listen again. Choose the correct answers.

The actor ...

1 is *American* / *Australian*.
2 has got *blue* / *brown* eyes.
3 has got two *brothers* / *sisters*.
4 has got *an Australian* / *a Spanish* wife.
5 has got *two daughters and a son* / *two sons and a daughter*.

8 Voice it! Discuss the questions.

1 Which information is interesting or surprising about this actor?
2 How are friends like family?

GRAMMAR IN ACTION

Have got questions

Watch video 1.3
Has she got blue eyes?
How many brothers has she got?

?	**Have** they **got** any children?	**Has** he **got** blue eyes?	How many brothers and sisters **has** he **got**?
+	Yes, they **have**.	Yes, he **has**.	He**'s got** two brothers.
–	No, they **haven't**.	No, he **hasn't**.	He **hasn't got** any sisters.

Grammar reference p124   Pronunciation p142

1 Write questions about Chris Hemsworth with the correct form of *have got*. Then ask and answer.

1 Chris / green eyes?
Has Chris got green eyes?
2 he / three brothers?
3 he / any sisters?
4 Chris and Elsa / a house in Australia?
5 they / three children?

1.10 **2** Write the questions and answers about the famous people, then guess the correct answer. Listen and check.

1 *How many brothers and sisters has Daniel Radcliffe got?*
a He's got one brother.
b He hasn't got any brothers or sisters.

3 COLLABORATE Work in pairs. Write three questions like the ones in Exercise 2 about famous people. Ask another pair. Can they guess the answer?

4 Use it! Ask the people in your class questions with the words in the box and write the names.

brown eyes   a twin brother or sister a pet   a mobile phone   long red hair freckles   a niece or nephew

Have you got brown eyes?

Yes, I have.

No, I haven't. I've got grey eyes.

5 Compare your answers with your classmates. What is interesting or surprising?

This week's STAR interview

We've got the questions.
Have you got the answers?

1 Q: How many / brothers and sisters / Daniel Radcliffe?
a one brother
b (✗) brothers or sisters

2 Q: Scarlett Johansson / a brother?
a a twin brother
b (✗) a twin sister

3 Q: Mila Kunis / green eyes?
a (✗) blue eyes
b (✗) one green eye and one brown eye

Finished? p21

SPEAKING
Phoning a friend

1 (1.11) **Listen to the conversation. Who is Jack?**

LILY: [1]… , Evan.
EVAN: Hi, Lily. Are you alright? [2]… ?
LILY: OK, thanks. [3]… ?
EVAN: [4]… , thanks. So, how's school?
LILY: It's good.
EVAN: Have you got any new friends?
LILY: Yes, I have. I've got one new friend. His name's Jack.
EVAN: Cool! I've got a new boy in my class. His name's Jack, too.
LILY: Has he got wavy black hair and blue eyes?
EVAN: Yes, he has. That's funny! Maybe it's the same boy. Imagine if it is!
LILY: That's so not funny, Evan!
EVAN: Got to go! [5]… !
LILY: OK, [6]… .

2 (1.11) **Complete the conversation with phrases from the *Useful language* box. Then listen again and check.**

Useful language

Bye! Hey, (Evan). Hi, (Lily). How are things?
OK/Fine, thanks. You? See you later.

3 **Look at the *Everyday English* box. How do you say these phrases in your language?**

Watch video 1.4
Everyday English

Are you alright? Cool! Got to go!
That's funny! That's so not funny!

4 **Lily and Evan use some of the phrases in the *Everyday English* box to react to each other. Can you think of any other phrases to do this?**

TASK
Plan your own phone conversation

PLAN

5 **Decide on the questions to ask your friend. Use the ideas below or your own ideas.**

school new friends family

SPEAK

6 **Practise the conversation.**

CHECKLIST **Remember to include:**
- *have got*
- the vocabulary from this unit
- the *Useful language* and *Everyday English* phrases.

CHECK

7 COLLABORATE **Work with another pair. Listen to their conversation and write examples of language they use from the CHECKLIST. Then say one interesting thing about your partner's conversation.**

Your *Connections!* friend is Martin. He's from England. Write to him below.

Hello Martin,

1 I'm Javi and this is my first email for the *Connections* project! I'm from Montijo, a small town in the west of Spain. I've got a big house and a very big family!

2 I've got six brothers and one sister. My brother, Dani, is my twin. He's tall. He's got short straight brown hair and brown eyes, like me. He's my brother and my friend! My sister, Claudia, is ten. She's got long brown hair and blue eyes and lots of freckles! I've got a pet rabbit. His name's Thumper! 🙂 🐇 My best friend's name is Toni. We're in the same class. He's funny! 😂

3 Here's a photo of me with Dani (he's got a red shirt) and Claudia. We're in my uncle's garden. My hair is very short in this photo.

4 Have you got a big family? Have you got any pets? Who's your best friend? 👍

Write soon!

Javi 👋

WRITING

An informal email

1 Look at the photo. Which boy is Javi? Read his email and find the answer.

2 Match topics a–d with paragraphs 1–4.

a Javi's questions for Martin
b Family and friends
c Introduction and reason for writing
d Extra information

3 Read the email again and answer the questions.

1 How old is Javi's sister?
2 How many brothers and sisters has Javi got?
3 Who is Thumper?
4 Who is Javi's best friend?

4 Complete the *Useful language* box with examples from Javi's email.

Useful language

at the start: Hi, Hey, [1]…
at the end: Email me soon, That's all for now, [2]… !
contractions: I'm, I've, [3]… , She's, [4]… , [5]… , Who's
symbols: use emojis to help express your feelings

TASK

Write an informal email to a new friend for the *Connections!* project

PLAN

5 Make notes about these things.

age family pets friend(s)

6 Decide what information to include.

At the start: Use an informal expression.
1: Introduction and reason for writing.
2: Describe your family and best friend(s).
3: Include extra information about a photo.
4: Ask questions.
At the end: Use an informal expression.

WRITE

7 Write your email.

CHECKLIST **Remember to include:**

- the verb *be* and the verb *have got*
- information about you and your family
- the *Useful language* phrases
- a photo of you and your family.

CHECK

8 COLLABORATE **Swap your email with a partner. Have they got the items in the** CHECKLIST**? Has your partner got a pet?**

Finished? p21

AROUND THE WORLD

READING

An article

1.12 **1 Look at the photos. Where are the people? What is special about them? Read and listen to the article to check your answers.**

2 Find words in the article that mean:

1. two children born at the same time (n.)
2. three children born at the same time (n.)
3. four children born at the same time (n.)
4. very young children (n.).

3 Read the article again. Choose the correct words.

1. The Festival of Twins is one *week* / *day* long.
2. Pleucadeuc isn't a *big* / *small* town.
3. The festival is for twins, triplets and quadruplets from *France* / *all over the world*.
4. Geoffrey and Guillaume *have got some* / *haven't got any* photos as babies at the Festival of Twins.

Globetrotters

Watch video 1.5
Children's Day

- What is Children's Day?
- When is Children's Day in Japan?
- Which city are the superheroes in?

4 Voice it! Answer the questions.

1. What is interesting about the Festival of Twins?
2. Have you got any twins in your family?
3. What do you think life is like as a twin?
4. Do you think traditions are important? Why / Why not?

Twins Day

France is the third biggest country in Europe and it's got a lot of different festivals. They've got a film festival in Cannes, music festivals in Paris and in Lyon, and there's a festival of lights!

But, perhaps one of the most unusual festivals of all is 'Deux et Plus' or 'Festival of Twins' on 15th August in the small town of Pleucadeuc in the northwest of France. More than 1,000 twins, triplets and quadruplets from all over the world meet in one place! Some look the same and some look different, some even speak their own language! Imagine that!

Explore it!

Guess the correct answer.

Identical twins have the same DNA, but they don't have the same …

a eye colour. **b** fingerprints. **c** hair colour.

Find two more interesting facts about twins. Choose your favourite fact and write a question for your partner to answer.

The festival has got its own traditions. Each twin, triplet, or quadruplet is usually in the same clothes with the same hairstyle! There are also a lot of interesting activities to do, like face painting, watching live music, dancing and playing fun games.

Geoffrey and Guillaume have got photos from their first visit to the festival of twins as babies. Now they are 13! 'It's a great day! We've got a lot of new friends this year.' Their new friends have all got the same DNA and one thing in common – they've all got brothers or sisters that look the same – or almost!!

LEARN TO LEARN

Increasing your vocabulary

When you learn an adjective, it's a good idea to learn the opposite adjective. Learning pairs of words together increases your vocabulary and helps you to remember words more easily.

5 Check the meaning of the adjectives in the box. Then find the opposite adjectives in the text.

big	last	normal	old

big – small

6 COLLABORATE Close your books. Say an adjective from Exercise 5. Can your partner remember the opposite adjective?

Mini culture project p128

1 REVIEW

VOCABULARY

1 **Look at Ruben's family tree. Complete the sentences.**

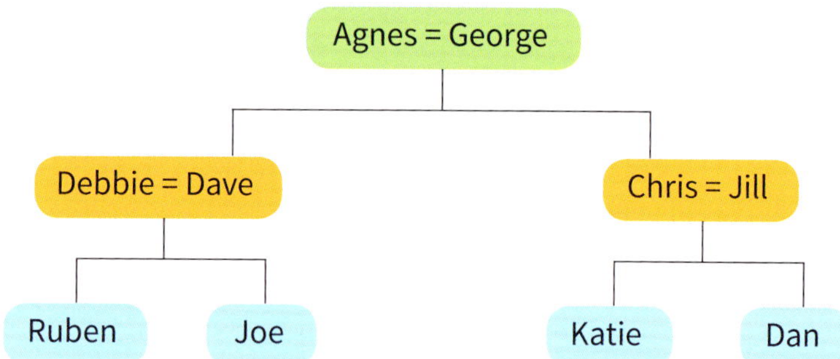

1 Joe: Agnes and George are my … .
2 Debbie and Dave: Ruben is our … .
3 Ruben: Katie and Dan are my … .
4 Jill: Ruben is my … .
5 Katie and Dan: Dave is our … .

2 **Complete the descriptions with words from the box.**

brown wavy glasses green
long red short short tall

Kirsty is [1]… .
She's got [2]… … … hair.
She's got [3]… eyes.

Jack is [4]… .
He's got short [5]… … hair.
He's got [6]… eyes.
He's got [7]… .

GRAMMAR

3 **Rewrite the sentences. Replace the underlined words with the words in brackets and 's or s'.**

1 Their names are Jack and Sara. (My parents)
2 Is that her phone? (Anna)
3 They're their bags. (my friends)
4 That's his bike. (Danny)

4 **Write the questions with *have got*. Then answer them with the information in brackets.**

1 how many / sisters / you (four)
2 Toby / any cousins (✗)
3 you / a big family (✓)
4 your best friend / a pet (✓) (two cats)
5 you / a phone / in your bag (✗)

Vocabulary

Family members

aunt
brother
cousin
dad
daughter
grandad
granddaughter
grandma
grandson
husband
mum
nephew
niece
sister
son
uncle
wife

Physical descriptions

Eyes: brown, grey
Hairstyle: long, short, wavy
Hair colour: blonde, brown, grey, red
Height: tall, short
Other features: beard, glasses, freckles, moustache

Grammar

Have got: affirmative, negative, questions and short answers
How many … ?
Possessive *'s*

1 FINISHED?

1 Write clues for the answers in the puzzle.

1 *Your mum or dad's brother is your . . .*

2 Look at the information. Write sentences about Harry and Amy with *has/have* (*not*) *got*. Then write a sentence about your family.

	Harry	Amy
1 sisters	0	2
2 brothers	3	0
3 cousins	6	9
4 nieces	0	0
5 nephews	3	2

1 *Harry hasn't got any sisters.*
Amy's got two sisters.

3 Follow the lines and write sentences. Use *It's* / *They're* and the possessive *'s* / *s'*.

1 *It's their parents' car*

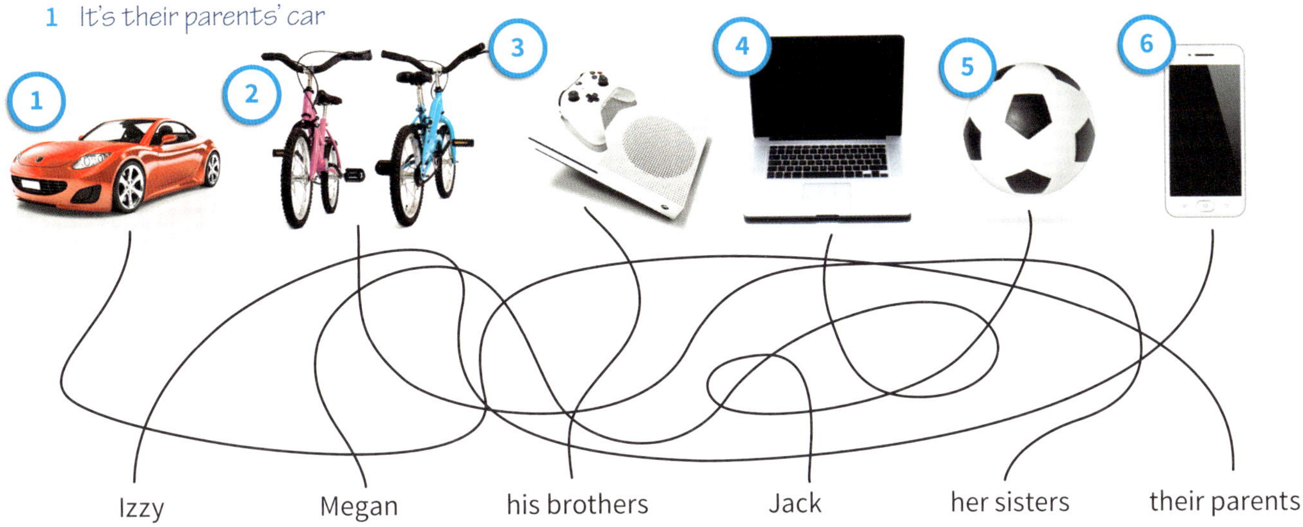

4 What differences can you see between the photos? Write as many sentences as you can in two minutes. Who are the people?

2 THAT'S LIFE!

LEARNING OUTCOMES

I can ...

- understand texts about daily routines
- ask and respond to interview questions
- write an article
- understand how to use the present simple and adverbs of frequency
- talk about daily routines and leisure activities
- identify word partners
- do a survey and present the results.

WATCH VIDEO 2.1

- Before you watch, is it day or night in India now?
- Watch and check. Which countries are in the video?
- Which is your favourite activity in the video? Why?

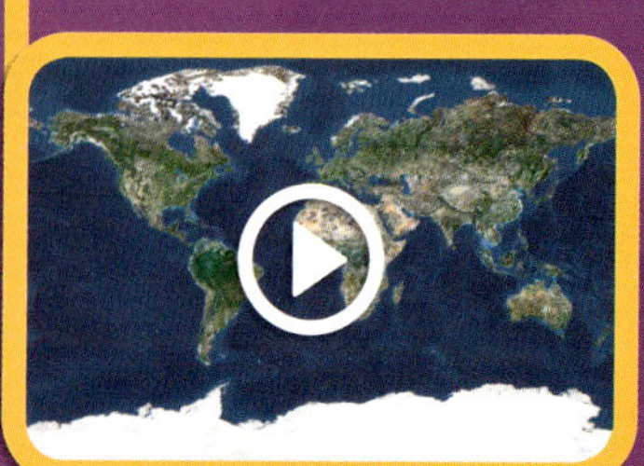

KICK-OFF! 2.1

p25

GRAMMAR IN ACTION 2.2

p27

GRAMMAR IN ACTION 2.3

p28

EVERYDAY ENGLISH 2.4

VOCABULARY

Daily routines

a

b

c

d

e

f

g

h

2.01 **1** Match eight of the activities in the box with the pictures a–h. Then listen, check and repeat.

brush your teeth check your phone do your homework ~~get dressed~~ get up go home go to bed go to school have a shower have breakfast pack your bag wake up

a *get dressed*

2.02 **2** Which activities in the box in Exercise 1 are not in the pictures? Put them in the correct order. Then listen, check and repeat.

2.03 **3** Listen to Eduardo talking about his day. Put all the activities from Exercise 1 in the correct order.

LEARN TO LEARN

Word partners (1)

When you learn new words, think about the words that go with them. This will help you to remember them.

4 Complete the table with activities from Exercise 1. Then think of one more for each verb.

Go	Get	Have
to school		

5 COLLABORATE Work in pairs. Take turns to say a verb from Exercise 4. Your partner says the activities that go with it.

6 **Use it!** Work in pairs. Take turns to say an activity from Exercise 1. Your partner guesses what time you do this activity.

have breakfast *7 o'clock?* *No, try again.*

Explore it!

Guess the correct answer.

When you brush your teeth and leave the tap on, you use … litres of water every minute.

a two b five c ten

Find an interesting fact about another daily routine. Then write a question for your partner to answer.

READING
A profile

A day in the life of ...

This is Amir from the Bajau tribe in Borneo. His life is unusual. He lives with his family in a house – but it's in the water. Amir doesn't know his age or the date of his birthday. The Bajau tribe don't count days and hours; they use the movement of the sea to count time.

Every morning, Amir wakes up early, but he doesn't have breakfast. He and his father go out in their boat. They swim in the water to look for food for the day. Amir and the people in his tribe can see really well under water. Amir catches a fish for breakfast and his father catches an octopus for dinner.

After breakfast, Amir usually meets his friends. They don't go to school and they don't study subjects like English. The older Bajau people teach them how to make nets and build boats.

In the afternoons, Amir and his friends dive into the water from bridges and they play in the water, too. It's their favourite place!

In the evenings, Amir's mother and sisters cook the octopus and then the family has dinner together. It's always delicious!

1 Tell your partner three things you do after breakfast.

2 Read and listen to the profile. Say one surprising thing about Amir's routine. (2.04)

3 Find words in the profile to match the photos.

a

b

c

d

4 Read the profile again and complete the sentences.

1. Amir lives in an unusual house with his family.
2. Amir and his father look for … every morning
3. The Bajau people can … really well under water.
4. Amir and his friends play in the water in the … .
5. Amir's favourite place is the … .

5 Are the sentences *T* (true) or *F* (false)?

1. Amir's house isn't in the water. F
2. Amir's family has got a boat.
3. Before breakfast, Amir is in the water.
4. Amir isn't happy in water.
5. Amir hasn't got any sisters.

6 Voice it! Discuss the questions.

1. How is Amir's life different from yours?
2. What do you like about Amir's day?

Finished? p33

Watch video 2.2
Name three things he does in the morning. Is he always on time for school?

GRAMMAR IN ACTION

Present simple: affirmative and negative

	I/You/We/They	*He/She/ It*
+	Amir and his father **go** out in their boat.	Amir **lives** with his family.
+	They **swim** in the water.	Amir **catches** a fish.
–	They **don't go** to school.	He **doesn't know** his age.

Grammar reference p124 Pronunciation p142

1 Correct the sentences. One sentence is correct. Which one? Check your answers with the profile on page 24.

1 Amir knows the date of his birthday.
Amir doesn't know the date of his birthday.
2 Amir and his father look for food together.
3 He plays with his friends in the evenings.
4 He and his friends study English.
5 He and his friends don't like the water.
6 He doesn't have dinner with his family in the evenings.

2.08 **2 Complete the text with the correct form of the present simple. Then listen and check.**

Nadia is 13 years old and she [1]*comes* (come) from Siberia. Her family is part of the Nenet tribe. They [2]… (not live) in the same place all year round. In summer, Nadia [3]… (travel) more than 1,000 km to the north of the country. She [4]… (not have got) a house. She [5]… (live) in a tent with her family. In winter, they [6]… (move) to the south of the country and their tent [7]… (go), too! How cool is that?

Adverbs of frequency

After breakfast, Amir **usually** meets his friends.
It's **always** delicious.

Grammar reference p127

3 Complete the chart with the adverbs of frequency.

often sometimes usually

4 Use it! **Imagine you are a famous person. Write three positive and three negative sentences with adverbs of frequency about your daily routine. Use the ideas in the box.**

do exercise do interviews have breakfast sing travel watch TV all afternoon

I always have breakfast in bed.

5 COLLABORATE **Swap your sentences with your partner. Guess who they are.**

Finished? p33

VOCABULARY AND LISTENING

Leisure activities

2.09 **1 Match the activities with the pictures. Listen, check and repeat.**

chat online   download songs   go for a bike ride
go shopping   hang out with friends   listen to music
make videos   play an instrument   play video games
read a book/magazine   take photos   ~~watch TV~~

1 *watch TV*

LEARN TO LEARN

Word partners (2)

When you learn new words, learn them together, not on their own. It's a good idea to learn them by topic area. This will help you remember them.

2 Write the activities from Exercise 1 under the headings.

Leisure activities

Indoors	Outdoors	Indoors and outdoors
play an instrument		

3 COLLABORATE **Work with a partner. Are your lists the same? Do you agree? Can you add any more?**

4 Change the words in bold to correct the sentences.

1 I usually **chat** music on my phone.
I usually listen to music on my phone.

2 We never **read** videos.

3 Victor **listens to** photos all the time!

4 Alex **downloads** online with his friends every evening.

5 Evie and Laura **take** the piano together.

5 Use it! **Work in groups to complete the sentences about how you spend your time. Use the activities from Exercise 1.**

All of us … None of us … Some of us …

All of us play video games at the weekend.

Street interviews

2.10 **6 Listen. Which activities from Exercise 1 do you hear?**

2.10 **7 Listen again. Choose the correct answers.**

1 Nina and her friends *like / don't like* the same music.

2 Nina *does / doesn't do* her homework before she chats online.

3 Nina *always / never* does her homework in the evenings.

4 Anton *plays / doesn't play* video games on his own.

5 George *lives / doesn't live* near Anton.

6 Anton *has got / hasn't got* a bike and a camera.

8 Work in pairs. Think about daily routines and leisure activities and write a timetable. Then tell another pair. Are your days similar?

GRAMMAR IN ACTION

Present simple: questions

Watch video 2.3
Where does Sophie live?
What does Max make?

	I/You/We/They	*He/She/It*
Yes/No	**Do** they **like** the same music?	Does your best friend live near you?
	Yes, they **do**. / No, they **don't**.	Yes, he **does**. / No, he **doesn't**.
Wh-	**What do** you **do**?	**Who does** Anton **play** with?
	We listen to music.	He usually **plays** with his best friend.
How often	**How often do** you **chat** online?	**How often does** she **do** that?
	Every evening.	Every day.

Grammar reference p124

1 **Put the words in the correct order to make questions. Then write the answers.**

1. Nina / hang out with friends / does ✓
   Does Nina hang out with friends?
   Yes, she does.
2. Nina and her friends / do / like / different music ✗
3. Nina / her homework / in the evenings / does / do ✓
4. Anton and George / play / do / video games together ✓
5. Anton / walk / to George's house / does ✗
6. Anton / take / a lot of photos / does ✓

2 **Use the ideas to write questions. Then ask and answer.**

1. play video games with friends (you)
   Do you play video games with friends?
   Yes, I do. / No, I don't.
2. give you homework every day (your English teacher)
3. live near you (your friends)
4. listen to music in the car (your parents)
5. get up early at the weekend (you)

Get it right!

Remember *do* and *does* in present simple questions.
Where does your best friend live? **NOT** ~~*Where your best friend live?*~~

Wh- questions

3 **Complete the questions with the words in the box.**

How often | What | What time | ~~When~~ | Where

1. *When* do you have breakfast?
2. … does your best friend live?
3. … do you get up on week days?
4. … do you do in your free time?
5. … does your English teacher give you homework?

4 **Ask and answer the questions in Exercise 3.**

5 **Use it!** **Make questions. Then ask and answer.**

1. What video games / you and your friends / like?
   What video games do you and your friends like?
2. Where / your best friend / live?
3. Who / you / meet / before school?

Finished? p33

3 SCHOOL DAYS

LEARNING OUTCOMES

I can ...

- understand texts about schools and school activities
- learn how to ask for help
- write a description of my ideal school
- understand how to use *can/can't* and *like*, *love*, etc. + *-ing*
- talk about school subjects and places in a school
- recognise cognates, make a spidergram and understand new words from context
- write a haiku.

WATCH VIDEO 3.1

- Before you watch, how do you go to school?
- Watch and check. What type of schools are there?
- Which school do you want to go to? Why?

KICK-OFF! 3.1

p37

GRAMMAR IN ACTION 3.2

p39

GRAMMAR IN ACTION 3.3

p40

EVERYDAY ENGLISH 3.4

p42

GLOBETROTTERS 3.5

VOCABULARY

School subjects

1 (3.01) **Match the school subjects with the pictures. Then listen, check and repeat.**

art design and technology (DT) drama English food technology geography history ~~maths~~ information and communication technology (ICT) music physical education (PE) science Spanish

a maths

2 **Choose the correct subjects.**

1 *Maths/Art* is my favourite subject. I love difficult sums.
2 I don't like *PE/food technology* when we go outside. I prefer it inside.
3 This year I want to study Shakespeare in *science/English*.
4 I never remember all the dates in *history/ICT*.
5 *Geography/English* isn't just about countries. It's also about population and people.
6 *Music/Spanish* is great this year. My word of the week is *gracias*.
7 My favourite part of *science/DT* is the experiments, but we don't do them every week.
8 We always have *registration/lunchtime* at the start of each day.

3 **Work with a partner. Ask and answer about your timetables. Talk about:**

subjects you're good a | your favourite subjects
subjects you're not good at | good/bad days

I'm good at PE. I'm not good at art. What about you?

LEARN TO LEARN

Recognising cognates

Lots of English words are similar to words in your language, but be careful! We don't always use them in the same way.

4 **Write the subjects from Exercise 1 under the headings.**

Similar to the names of subjects in my language	Very different from the names of subjects in my language

5 COLLABORATE **Close your books. How many words from Exercise 1 can you remember? How many of these words are similar to the names of subjects in your language? Can you add any more subjects?**

6 **Use it!** **Write five definitions for school subjects. Can your partner guess the subjects?**

You draw and paint in this subject. *Art!*

Explore it!

Guess the correct answer.

In Australia, students have six weeks' *summer / winter* holiday from mid-December to the end of January.

Find an interesting fact about schools. Then write a question for your partner to answer.

READING

A webpage

Ballet School

Rumba, mambo, and salsa are just some of the dance styles that come from Cuba, and dancers are big stars in Cuba. The Cuban National Ballet School in Havana **trains** boys and girls to do **ballet** and many of the students become the world's **top** ballet dancers.

Children usually start at the school when they are ten years old, for five years of training. Then they sometimes train for three and a half more years at a professional level.

The school day starts at 7.00 am and finishes at 7.00 pm. That's a 12-hour day! And some students go to school before classes start to do exercises! In the morning students study subjects like history, maths, languages, science and music. At lunchtime they can have a break, but they can't go home. In the afternoons, they dance.

Oscar is a student there. 'It's **tough** and sometimes I just want to do nothing. I can dance and read music quite well, but I can't play the piano at all. My best friend Carlos can dance very well. He can sing well, too, but I can't – I sing badly! One day, I want to be a dancer like my **hero**, Javier Rojas.'

Learning to be a top ballet dancer is really hard work! Are you tough enough?

1 Look at the photos and read the title. What do you want to know about the webpage?

2 (3.02) Read and listen to the webpage. Close your books. Write two things you remember about it.

3 Find the words in **bold** in the webpage and then choose the correct option.

1. Ballet *isn't* / *is* a type of dance.
2. Top is to be number *one* / *two*.
3. Tough is something *easy* / *difficult*.
4. Hero is a person you think is *great* / *not very good*.
5. Train is to *prepare yourself for* / *think about* an activity.

4 Read the webpage again and complete the sentences.

1. The Cuban National Ballet School is in Havana.
2. Lots of the students become world-famous … .
3. Most students start training at the school when they are … .
4. Some students … in the morning before classes start.
5. Students can have a break at … .
6. In the afternoons, students … .

5 Voice it! Discuss the questions.

1. Has your country got schools like Oscar's school? What type?
2. What are the similarities and the differences between your school and Oscar's?
3. Do you want to go to a ballet school like Oscar? Why / Why not?

Finished? p45

Watch video 3.2
Can he speak another language?
Can anyone become a vlogger?

GRAMMAR IN ACTION

Can for ability and permission

	I/You/He/She/It/We/They	
+	Ability: I **can** dance.	Permission: At lunchtime they **can** have a break.
–	Ability: Oscar **can't** play the piano.	Permission: Students **can't** go home at lunchtime.
?	Ability: **Can** Oscar sing well? Yes, he can. / No, he can't.	**Can** they dance well? Yes, they can. / No, they can't.

Grammar reference p124 Pronunciation p142

1 Choose the correct option. Then check your answers in the webpage on page 36.

1 Oscar (*can*) / *can't* read music.
2 Oscar *can* / *can't* sing well.
3 Carlos *can* / *can't* sing well.
4 Javier Rojas *can* / *can't* dance well.

2 Remember the information from the webpage and complete the sentences.

very well | well | quite well
not at all | badly | not very well

1 Oscar can read music … .
2 He can't play the piano … .
3 Carlos can dance … .
4 Oscar can sing … .

3 Complete the text with the correct form of *can*. Then listen and check. (3.06)

Get it right!

We use the verb without *to* after *can*.

Vicki can sing **NOT** ~~*Vicki can to sing*~~

4 Use it! Write sentences about things you can or can't do and how well or badly you do them. Use the ideas below or your own ideas.

count to ten in a different language   do ballet
sing a song in Russian   write music

I can't do ballet at all but I can dance well.

5 COLLABORATE Ask and answer questions. Find one thing you and your partner can both do well and one thing you can't do at all.

Can you count to ten in a different language?

Yes, I can. I can count to ten in English very well.

A day in Huaho school

Huaho school in Finland is different. Can you guess why?

Students ¹*can choose* (choose) the subjects they want to study. Teachers ²… (tell) them what to do. Students ³… (use) their mobiles in class to do research. ⁴… (you / do) that in your school?

Students and teachers ⁵… (take) a break after every lesson. They ⁶… (chat) to friends or go outside.

Students ⁷… (do) homework. Why? Because the teachers don't give them any!
⁸… (you / imagine) a school like this?

Finished? p45

VOCABULARY AND LISTENING

Places in a school

3.07 **1** Match the words with places 1–12 in the plan. Listen, check and repeat.

canteen classroom ICT room library
locker area main hall playing field ~~reception~~
science lab sports hall staffroom toilets

1 *canteen*

3.08 **2** Listen and write the seven places you hear.

LEARN TO LEARN

Making a spidergram

Try to think of other words related to new words and make spidergrams to increase your vocabulary.

3 Choose places in your school from Exercise 1. Write down other words related to them.

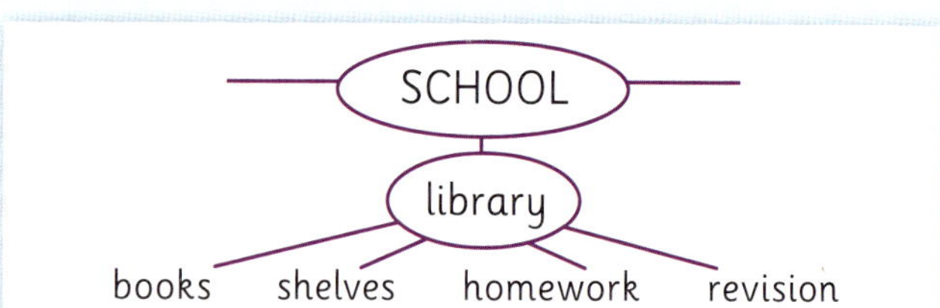

4 COLLABORATE Compare your words with a partner. Are your words the same or different? Add more new words.

5 Use it! Ask and answer about the places in your school. Use as many words as you can from Exercises 1 and 3.

Where do you do homework?

I do my homework in the library. What about you?

A radio programme

3.09 **6** Listen. What is the radio programme about?

3.09 **7** Listen again. Choose the correct answers.

1 The club is usually in the *main hall / library*.
2 The club meets once a *week / month*.
3 The club *starts / finishes* at 3.15.
4 Mrs McKenzie is Lidia's *drama / English* teacher.
5 Max lives *near / far from* the school.

8 Voice it! Discuss the questions.

1 What kinds of books do you like?
2 Have you got a book club at your school?
3 Which clubs do you go to? When and where are they?

GRAMMAR IN ACTION

Verb forms: (don't) like, don't mind, love, hate + -ing

Watch video 3.3
What's her favourite subject?
What does she love doing?

We all **love reading** books. 😊😊😊	I **don't mind staying** for the book club. 😐
We **like talking** about them, too. 😊	Some of my friends **hate reading**. ☹☹☹
I **don't like going** to after-school clubs. ☹	

Grammar reference p127

1 **Complete the sentences. Which ones are correct?**

1 Lidia *loves reading* (read) books. 😊😊😊 ✓
2 The students at the book club … (talk) about books. ☹
3 Max usually … (go) to after-school clubs. ☹☹☹
4 Max … (stay) for this club. 😐
5 All of Max's friends … (read). 😊

2 **Write true sentences. Use the verb forms and the ideas in the box or your own ideas.**

do homework with friends   get up early   hang out with friends   learn new vocabulary   listen to rap music   read a book at the weekend   revise for exams   take photos

I like doing homework with friends.

3 **Ask and answer. Find three things you have in common.**

Do you like getting up early?

No! I hate getting up early. What about you?

I don't mind getting up early on week days.

Object pronouns

We use object pronouns after a verb or preposition to replace nouns and to avoid repeating the same word.

Grammar reference p126

4 **Match the object pronouns with the people or things.**

1 Lidia's here with **me**.
2 We like talking about **them**, too!
3 We have English with **her**.
4 What's **it** about?

a books
b the radio presenter
c Lidia's book
d Mrs McKenzie

5 **Complete the sentences.**

1 Is Logan in this class? I want to talk to *him*.
2 Our teacher always gives … a lot of homework.
3 Where are Jessica and Mehmet? Let's call … now.
4 The seat next to Jenny is free. You can sit next to … .
5 Is this your dictionary? Can I borrow …, please?

6 **Use it!** **Think about things you like and don't like at your school. Compare your ideas with a partner. Agree on changes you want to make.**

I don't like eating in the canteen. The food isn't good.

I agree. Let's change our routine on Mondays. We can cook lunch at home at the weekend and bring it to school.

7 **Present your favourite idea to the class with your partner. The class chooses the best idea.**

Finished? p45

4 YOU ARE WHAT YOU EAT

LEARNING OUTCOMES

I can ...

- understand texts about food
- order in a snack bar
- write a description of my favourite food
- understand how to use countable and uncountable nouns and *There is/are*
- talk about and describe food
- personalise vocabulary and answer true/false questions
- design a food truck and evaluate a design project.

WATCH VIDEO 4.1

- Before you watch, name three types of food.
- Watch and check. How many types of bread are there?
- Do you like cooking?

KICK-OFF! 4.1

p51

GRAMMAR IN ACTION 4.2

p53

GRAMMAR IN ACTION 4.3

p54

EVERYDAY ENGLISH 4.4

VOCABULARY
Food and drink

1 Write all the food and drink words you know in English. Compare with a partner. How many words have you got?

2 4.01 Match the words in the box with the photos. Then listen, check and repeat.

apples	bananas	beans	carrots	cheese
chicken	~~chocolate~~	eggs	fish	fizzy drink
juice	meat	rice	water	

a *chocolate*

LEARN TO LEARN

Personalising vocabulary

It's a good idea to think about your own routines and habits when you learn new vocabulary. This can help you to remember the words.

3 When do you have the food and drinks in Exercise 2? Write the words in the table.

Breakfast	Lunch	Dinner

4 COLLABORATE Compare with a partner. Write sentences about your partner's meals. Use *always*, *usually*, *often*, *sometimes* or *never*.

Eva always has an egg and juice for breakfast.

Get it right!

We say *I don't like apples.* **NOT** ~~*I don't like the apples.*~~

5 Use it! Discuss the questions.

1 Which food do you love/hate?

2 Which food do you eat when you're happy? What about when you're sad?

Explore it!

Guess the correct answer.

One hundred grams of ants have got …

a less protein than an egg

b more protein than an egg

c the same protein as an egg.

Find an interesting fact about food. Then write a question for your partner to answer.

Time for a snack

a

Leakena is from Cambodia. She hasn't got a banana for a snack today, she's got a spider. She usually buys one tarantula from a food stall on the way home from school. 'You cook them in **oil** and then add some **salt** and some sugar. They're like chicken or fish. The legs are my favourite!'

b

Kgosi is from Botswana in southern Africa. He hasn't got any apples today, but he's got some Mopane worms. 'I like sharing them with friends at school. They're great with some **peanut butter** or some rice and they've got more protein than meat. I haven't got any rice today, just 50 worms!'

c

Jorge is from Oaxaca, Mexico. He's got some chocolate today but he's also got a grasshopper taco. 'My mum cooks grasshoppers in some oil and she always adds some **garlic**. They're my favourite snack and I sometimes buy them at the market'. Bugs like grasshoppers, spiders, and worms are good for you and the planet. They give us protein and they aren't expensive to feed. Which bug do you want to try?

READING

An article

1 **Look at the photos of food in the article. Where do you think people eat this food? Do they enjoy it?**

2 (4.02) **Read and listen to the article and check your answers to Exercise 1.**

3 **Check the meaning of the words in bold in the article.**

4 **Choose the correct answer. Which person ...**

Leakena Kgosi Jorge

1 enjoys sharing snacks with friends? Kgosi
2 usually buys a snack after school?
3 enjoys the snack at home with garlic and oil?
4 likes eating the snack with rice?
5 has got two types of snack today?
6 likes eating a bug's legs?

5 Voice it! **Discuss the questions.**

1 Do people in your country eat bugs?
2 Which of these bugs do you want to try?
3 Why do you think eating bugs is good for the planet?

Finished? p59

GRAMMAR IN ACTION

Countable and uncountable nouns

Watch video 4.2
What food can you see at the market?
What's his favourite food?

Countable nouns	Uncountable nouns
Some nouns are countable: you can count them. *one tarantula, 50 worms, a taco, an apple*	Other nouns are uncountable: you can't count them. *chocolate, salt, sugar, meat, garlic*

Grammar reference p127

1 Put the words in the box in the correct circle.

beans bread carrots cheese eggs fish juice meat milk rice tomatoes

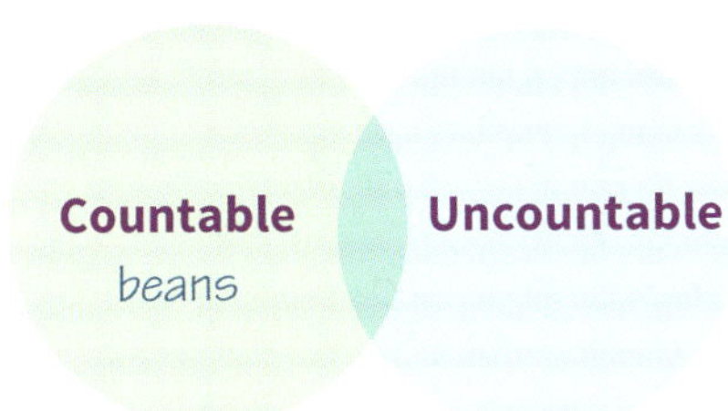

2 COLLABORATE Work with a partner. Add more food words to the circles in Exercise 1. How many have you got?

A/an, some/any

	Singular countable	Plural countable	Uncountable
+	Leakena's got **a** spider.	Kgosi's got **some** worms.	Jorge's got **some** chocolate today.
–	She hasn't got **a** banana.	He hasn't got **any** apples.	Kgosi hasn't got **any** rice today.
?	Have you got **a** spider?	Have you got **any** worms?	Have you got **any** chocolate?

Grammar reference p127

4.03 **3** Complete the conversation with *a*, *an*, *some* or *any*. Then listen and check.

CELIA: Have we got [1]any food for the party?
OSCAR: Let's have a look. Right, we've got [2]… cheese.
CELIA: OK. Have we got [3]… bread?
OSCAR: Sorry. We haven't got [4]… bread but we've got [5]… pasta.
CELIA: Have we got [6]… fruit or vegetables?
OSCAR: We've got [7]… apple and [8]… carrot.
CELIA: What about drinks?
OSCAR: We've got [9]… water.
CELIA: Great. What a party! I can't wait.

4 Use it! Work with a partner. Change the food and drink words in Exercise 3 and write your own conversation. Practise your conversation.

5 COLLABORATE Listen carefully to other conversations. Which party do you want to go to?

Finished? p59

VOCABULARY AND LISTENING

Adjectives

4.04 **1** Complete the sentences with the adjectives in the box. Listen and check.

cold	delicious	disgusting	fresh	healthy
hot	nice	salty	sweet	~~unhealthy~~

1

Fizzy drinks aren't good for you but I sometimes drink them. I know they're unhealthy.

2

Careful! The soup is ... .

3

Peanuts have got salt on them. They're ..., but they aren't bad for you.

4

I really hate cheese. I don't know how people can eat it, I think it's ... .

5

These beetles taste great! They're ... .

6

Yuk! This milk doesn't smell ... . I don't want any in my coffee.

7

Dark chocolate hasn't got much sugar in it. It isn't ... but I love it!

8

I never eat ice cream in winter. The weather is ... and so is ice cream!

9

The vegetables and fruit in our garden are always ... and they're a very ... snack.

4.05 **2** Listen to the words in Exercise 1 and repeat them. Which two words have got a negative meaning?

> Pronunciation p142

3 **Use it!** Write two adjectives to describe a type of food. Tell a partner. Can they guess?

They're disgusting and salty.

Are they spiders?

A quiz

LEARN TO LEARN

True or false sentences

With true or false sentences, you've got a 50% chance of being correct! Before you listen, read the sentences then change them into questions and try to predict if the sentences are true or false. This helps you to listen for the correct information.

4 COLLABORATE Change the sentences in Exercise 5 to questions. Then predict if sentences 2–4 are *T* (true) or *F* (false).

1 *How many peanuts are there in a jar of peanut butter?*

4.09 **5** Listen to the quiz and check. How many of your predictions are correct?

durian

cocoa

carmine

1 There are 1,000 peanuts in a jar of peanut butter. F
2 You can't eat durians on public transport.
3 White chocolate isn't really chocolate.
4 Carmine is an orange powder from beetles.
5 Theo answers all the questions correctly.

6 **Voice it!** Discuss the questions.

1 Do you want to try a durian?
2 Do you like orange fizzy drinks? Is your opinion the same after listening?

GRAMMAR IN ACTION

There is/isn't, there are/aren't

Watch video 4.3
What food has she got in her house?
How many hours does she sleep?

	Countable singular	Uncountable	Countable plural
+	**There's** a quiz in this magazine.	**There's** some water in the fridge.	**There are** 540 peanuts in a jar.
–	**There isn't** a quiz in the magazine.	**There isn't** any water.	**There aren't** any oranges in this drink.
?	**Is there** a quiz in the magazine?	Is **there** any water?	**Are there** five questions in the quiz?
Short answer	**Yes, there is.** / **No there isn't.**	**Yes, there is.** / **No there isn't.**	**Yes, there are.** / **No, there aren't.**

Grammar reference p124

4.10 **1** Choose the correct words. Listen and check.

ALI: I'm hungry! Let's make some chicken and rice.
BEN: We can't! There [1]*is* / *isn't* any rice.
ALI: OK. What about an omelette? [2]*There are* / *Are there* any eggs?
BEN: [3]*There's* / *There are* only one!
ALI: Oh dear! [4]*There is* / *Is there* any pasta?
BEN: No, there [5]*is* / *isn't*.
ALI: [6]*Is* / *Are* there any potatoes? Let's make chips!
BEN: No, there [7]*are* / *aren't*. There [8]*isn't* / *aren't* any food in the house!
ALI: [9]*There's* / *There are* a food market today. Let's go!
BEN: OK. Oh no – I haven't got any money!

2 Look at the picture and complete the questions with *Is there* or *Are there*.

1 any fruit?
Is there any fruit?
2 any vegetables?
3 any juice?
4 a sandwich?
5 any eggs?
6 any fish?
7 any tomatoes?

3 Ask and answer the questions in Exercise 2.

Is there any fruit? *Yes, there is.*

Much/many, a lot of

	Countable plural	Uncountable
+	There are **a lot of** peanuts in a jar of peanut butter.	I've got **a lot of** homework.
–	There aren't **many** questions in the quiz.	I haven't got **much** time.
?	**How many** questions are there?	**How much** time have you got?

Grammar reference p127

4 Write questions with *How much* / *many*.

1 fruit / do you eat / every day?
How much fruit do you eat every day?
2 people / are there / in your family?
3 books / do you read / in a year?
4 water / do you drink / at school?
5 lessons / have got / on Friday?
6 time / spend / with friends at the weekend?
7 snacks / eat / every day?
8 money / have got / in your pocket today?

5 **Use it!** Ask and answer the questions in Exercise 4.

Finished? p59

SPEAKING

Ordering food and drink

4.11 **1** Listen to the conversation. What does Gulay choose from The Juice Stop?

JUST JUICES: £4.00

THE JUICE STOP

Fresh and Natural

Sunshine Start
Start your day with a delicious mix of fruit and vegetables.

Green Giant
Gives you energy with fresh green vegetables and there's an apple, too!

Fresh Lemorange
3 oranges, 2 lemons, some fizzy water and our secret ingredient.

WATER STOP: £1.50
Fizzy water

SNACK STATION: £0.75
Apple, Banana, Carrot

If you can't see what you want, don't worry. Ask and we can make it just for you. Tap water is free!

SERVER: Hi. [1]… ?
GULAY: [2]… juice, please.
SERVER: No problem. [3]… ?
GULAY: I'm not sure. [4]… Sunshine Start?
SERVER: There are two oranges, a carrot and three tomatoes in that one. It's really healthy.
GULAY: Hmm. What about the Green Giant? That sounds delicious.
SERVER: There are some green beans and a green apple in that.
GULAY: Thanks. [5]… some fizzy water and an apple?
SERVER: Of course. No worries! [6]… ?
GULAY: Yes, it is. Thank you. [7]… ?
SERVER: [8]… £2.25, … .
GULAY: Here you go.
SERVER: Thanks. Enjoy!
GULAY: Thank you. Bye!

4.11 **2** Complete the conversation with phrases from the *Useful language* box. Then listen again and check.

Useful language

Can I have … ?	Is that everything?
Can I help you?	That's … , please.
How much is that?	What kind?
I'd like a/an/some …	What's in the … ?

3 Look at the *Everyday English* box. How do you say these phrases in your language?

Watch video 4.4
Everyday English

Enjoy! Here you go.
No problem. No worries!

4 Who uses the *Everyday English* expressions: Gulay or the server?

TASK

Plan your own conversation

PLAN

5 Work with a partner. Decide on the following things.

where you are
who is the server and who is the customer
what's on the menu
how much money the customer has got
what to choose from the menu

SPEAK

6 Practise the conversation.

CHECKLIST **Remember to include:**

- *There is(n't) / There are(n't)* and *How much/many*
- the vocabulary from this unit
- the *Useful language* and *Everyday English* phrases.

CHECK

7 COLLABORATE **Work with another pair. Listen to their conversation and write examples of language they use from the** CHECKLIST. **What food have they got?**

WRITING

A description

My favourite food

by João Pereira

1 My name's João and I'm from Recife in Brazil. Here are some photos of my favourite types of food. I often have these at the weekend.

2 My dad makes cheese bread for breakfast. There's a lot of cheese in it. It's nice and I eat it when it's hot!

3 I usually buy lunch from a food stall or a shop. There are a lot of food stalls in my part of town and it isn't difficult to find delicious food! We often have chicken xim xim. It's very healthy. It's chicken with rice and there are a lot of peanuts. They're salty but they're nice.

4 I love chocolate balls. I always buy them after lunch from Thiago's stall. They're very sweet. I love eating them with my hands but I can't eat more than two or three. They're definitely my favourite snack!

1 **Look at the photos. What do you think the food is? Read the description and check.**

2 **Match topics a–d with paragraphs 1–4.**

a Snacks
b Introduction: who you are, what the description is about
c Breakfast
d Lunch

3 **Find examples of *and*, *but* and *or* in João's description. Complete the information in the *Useful language* box.**

Useful language

We use [1]… to add similar information.
We use [2]… to contrast different information
We use [3]… when there is a choice (usually between two things).

TASK

Write a description of your favourite types of food

PLAN

4 **Make notes about your favourite types of food.**

1: Introduction: give your name, where you are from, when / how often you eat your favourite foods.

2: Describe the first type of food: who makes it and what it's like.

3: Describe your other favourite food: where you buy/eat it, who you eat it with, what's in it, what it's like.

4: Describe your favourite snack, where you buy it, when you eat it and how you eat it.

WRITE

5 **Write your description.**

CHECKLIST **Remember to include:**

- *there is/are* and countable and uncountable nouns
- adjectives to describe the food
- the information from Exercise 4
- four paragraphs
- *and*, *but*, *or*.

CHECK

6 COLLABORATE **Swap your descriptions with a partner. Have they got the items in the** CHECKLIST**? What is their favourite food?**

Finished? p. 59

THE ART PROJECT

Design a food truck

1 Discuss the questions.

1 What food do you buy in the street or from food trucks?
2 When do people buy food from a food truck?
3 Are there any food trucks near where you live?

2 Look at the design for a food truck and answer the questions.

1 What kind of food do you think it sells? *Caribbean food.*
2 What kind of soup is there?
3 What is there to eat with the meat?
4 How much does today's special cost?
5 What sweet food can you buy?
6 What is the special offer?

3 Work with a partner. Choose the food you want to order from the food truck. Compare with another pair. Do you choose the same things?

How to evaluate a design

4.12

4 What do you think are the most important things in a design project? Choose from the list. Then listen and check.

a design b content c punctuation
d grammar e paragraphs f spelling

5 How well do you think the *Caribbean Sunshine* project presents the things in the table? Use the key to evaluate them.

Information		Design	
Name		Menu presentation	
Type of food		Pictures	
Food and drinks		Colours	
Prices			

Key
Excellent ✓✓✓✓
Very good ✓✓✓
Good ✓✓
Developing ✓

TASK

Design your own food truck

PLAN

6 **Work in groups. Choose the theme for your food truck. Then complete the steps below.**

- Choose a name for your food truck.
- Decide on the design and illustrations for it.
- Decide and agree on the food you want to sell.
- Decide and agree on the prices.
- Plan and design the menu.
- Draw and illustrate your food truck.

PRESENT

7 **Display your food truck design on your classroom wall. Don't forget to include the items in the CHECKLIST.**

CHECKLIST **Remember to include:**

- an interesting menu
- well organised information
- an attractive design
- the tips in *How to* evaluate a design.

CHECK

8 COLLABORATE **Look at your classmates' designs. Do they use the items in the CHECKLIST? Evaluate their designs and choose your favourite.**

5 WHAT'S YOUR STYLE?

LEARNING OUTCOMES

I can ...

- understand texts about fashion and a Hindu wedding
- buy clothes and accessories
- write a description of a photo
- understand how to use present tenses
- talk about clothes and accessories
- make a picture dictionary and practise vocabulary by making connections
- create a lookbook.

WATCH VIDEO 5.1

- Before you watch, which people wear uniforms?
- Watch and check. Have all schools got uniforms?
- Do you think uniforms are a good idea?

KICK-OFF! 5.1

p63

GRAMMAR IN ACTION 5.2

p65

GRAMMAR IN ACTION 5.3

p66

EVERYDAY ENGLISH 5.4

p68

GLOBETROTTERS 5.5

VOCABULARY

Clothes

5.01 **1** Match the words in the box with the pictures. Then listen, check and repeat.

boots cap hoodie jacket jeans joggers flip-flops trainers T-shirt skirt shirt ~~shorts~~

a *shorts*

2 Which look do you prefer? Why? Compare with a partner. Do you like the same looks?

3 Choose the odd one out.

1 skirt / jeans/ joggers / shorts
2 flip-flops / trainers / shirt / boots
3 shorts / jacket / hoodie
4 shirt / hoodie / jeans / T-shirt
5 jacket / cap / shirt / hoodie

LEARN TO LEARN

Making a picture dictionary

Drawing and labelling pictures is a good way to help you remember new vocabulary.

4 Make your own picture dictionary for the clothes in Exercise 1. Compare with a partner.

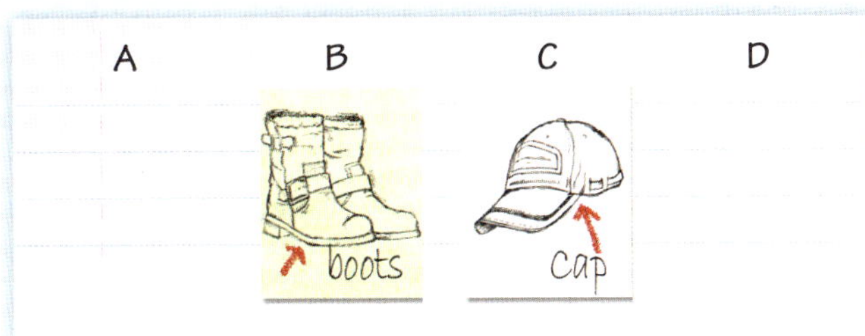

5 COLLABORATE Add more pictures to your dictionary. Cover the labels and show them to a partner. Can they guess the words?

6 Use it! Discuss the questions.

1 What do you wear to school / at the weekend?
2 What is your favourite outfit? Why?
3 What do you never wear?

Explore it!

Guess the correct answer.

Flip-flops have a lot of different names around the world. What do people in New Zealand call them?

a slops b jandals c chinelos

What do you call them? Find an interesting clothes fact. Then write a question for your partner to answer.

READING
An online diary

1 Look at the photos and describe the clothes you see. Where do you think the people are from?

5.02 2 Read and listen to the online diary and check your answer to Exercise 1.

3 Choose the correct answer. Which person …

Michiko Sofia Akiko

1 has got a pet? Michiko
2 has got a maths test?
3 is Michiko's friend?
4 is wearing boots?
5 is wearing sandals?
6 wants to go outside?

4 Find two adjectives in the online diary for the headings then think of two more adjectives for each heading.

Colour: black, …

Size:

Style:

5 Voice it! Discuss the questions.

1 Do you dress like your friends? Why / Why not?
2 How do the people you like influence the clothes you wear?
3 How does the place you live in influence the clothes you wear?

Michiko'sMix.com

Saturday, 8 am

HAPPY WEEKEND!

I'm writing this post in my bedroom. My little cat, Candy, is sleeping right here beside me.

What are you doing this morning? It's so hot!

Comments

10 replies ❤ 12 likes

Sofia: Hi, Michiko. I'm revising for a maths test! ☹ It's really hot and I want to be outside!

Michiko: Poor you! Good luck! My friend is calling me. See you later!

10 AM (and back online!)

We ❤ Harajuku – the fashion district

I'm sitting in a café with my best friend, Akiko. We're mixing traditional Japanese clothes with our own clothes to create a wamono style today. Look! We're wearing summer dresses and shirts. I'm wearing big black boots but Akiko isn't wearing the same boots. She's wearing zori (they're Japanese sandals).

We're also people watching from the café! There are a lot of different looks. There's a boy outside the café. He's wearing a black and white striped T-shirt, a red shirt, tight jeans, a green jacket and trainers. What a cool retro sporty look! What do you think?

Comments

Kyle from London: I love it!

1 PM Lunch time

I'm not having ramen today. I've got sushi and sashimi. It's definitely a susimi kind of day. Delicious! Are you having ramen for lunch?

Comments:

Lily: No, I'm not. I'm making pizza for ten friends!

Finished? p71

GRAMMAR IN ACTION

Present continuous

Watch video 5.2
What is he wearing?
Is Hiro wearing a uniform?

	I	*He/She/It*	*We/You/They*
+	**I'm writing** this post in my bedroom.	Akiko **is wearing** Japanese sandals.	We**'re mixing** traditional Japanese clothes.
–	**I'm not having** ramen today.	Akiko **isn't wearing** black boots.	Michiko and Akiko **aren't wearing** the same boots.
?	Am I writing this in my bedroom?	**Is** Sofia **revising** this morning?	**What are** you **doing** this morning?
	Yes, I **am**. / No, I**'m not.**	Yes, **she is**. / No, **she isn't**.	**Are** you **having** ramen today? Yes, I **am**. / No, **I'm not**.

Grammar reference p124 Pronunciation p142

1 **Complete the posts with the present continuous form of the verbs.**

What [1]*are* you *doing* (do)?

- I [2]… (draw) my own design on my T-shirt. I [3]… (create) my own style. 🙂 *Emy*
- I [4]… (not sit) on the beach today because it [5]… (rain) but I [6]… (wear) flip-flops. *Felipe*
- I [7]… (not wear) flip-flops but that's a good idea! *Sergio*
- We [8]… (dance) in my bedroom. Some of my friends [9]… (take) photos and they [10]… (post) them now. Take a look! *Luiza*

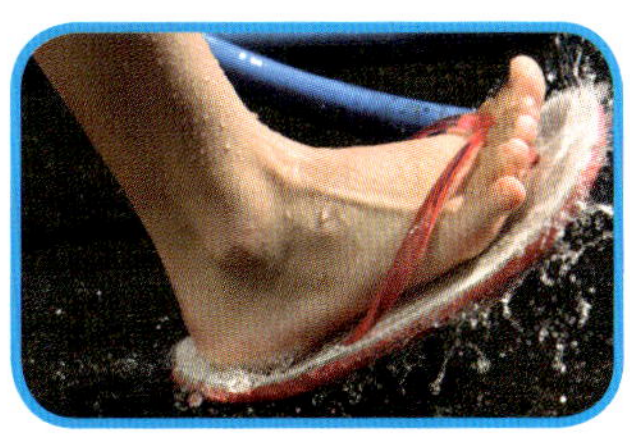

2 **Remember the information from the online diary. Write sentences in the present continuous. Check with a partner. How many sentences have you got?**

Get it right!

We say: *Are you wearing a cap?* **NOT** ~~*You are wearing a cap?*~~

3 COLLABORATE **Choose a classmate but don't tell your partner. Then ask questions to guess your partner's classmate. Ask ten questions. Your partner can only answer *Yes* or *No*!**

Is this person sitting near me?

No.

4 **Use it!** **Write present continuous questions. Then ask and answer with a partner.**

1 what / you / wear / today?
2 which TV series / you / watch / this month?
3 where / your best friend / sit?
4 what / you / think about / right now?

Finished? p71

AROUND THE WORLD

READING

A magazine article interview

1 Look at the photo. Discuss the questions.

1 Where do you think the people are from?
2 What do you think they are celebrating?
3 What is the woman at the front holding?

2 5.09 Read and listen to the interview and check your answers to Exercise 1.

3 Read the interview again and answer the questions.

1 How long does a Hindu wedding last for?
2 What is a lehenga?
3 What colour is popular for Hindu weddings? Why?
4 What accessories is Mishal wearing in the photo?
5 What is a sherwani?

4 Copy and complete the table with adjectives ending in *-ful* from the interview. Check the meanings in a dictionary.

Noun	Adjective
1 wonder	wonderful
2 colour	
3 beauty	
4 power	

5 Voice it! Answer the questions.

1 1 What do people wear to special celebrations in your country?
2 What is a typical wedding like in your country?
3 Are colours important in your country? Have they got special meanings?

Special Days

Weddings are a wonderful time for families and friends to celebrate together and to wear special clothes. This week, Amrit is talking about his cousin's Hindu wedding in India and some of their traditions.

Q: What are Hindu weddings like?
A: They're incredible! There's a lot of amazing food, music and dancing. They're always very colourful events because everyone wears beautiful clothes. They last for three days.

Q: What does the bride wear?
A: The bride usually wears a lehenga (a long skirt with a top) and a long scarf. Red is very popular at Hindu weddings. It's a powerful colour because in India it symbolises love and new life. In this photo, my cousin Mishal is wearing a red and gold lehenga. She's also wearing special wedding accessories: a gold necklace, earrings, rings on her fingers and toes, and lots of red and gold bracelets.

Globetrotters

Watch video 5.5
Cultural Fashion

- Where do the 'blue people' live?
- What do the Sami make?
- Which colour is important for the Maasai?

Q: What does the groom wear?

A: The groom usually wears a sherwani (a long jacket with gold designs on it), a pair of trousers and special wedding shoes. My cousin's new husband, Ranjit, is also wearing a red turban.

Q: Are there are any other special wedding traditions?

A: There are lots, but my favourite is joota chupai – a member of the bride's family steals the groom's wedding shoes and hides them. It's great fun! In this photo, my aunt Jaz is holding Ranjit's shoes and everyone is laughing.

People around the world celebrate special days like weddings and birthdays in different ways. How do you celebrate special days in your country?

Explore it!

Guess the correct answer.

Hindu brides have special paint on their hands. What does the paint include in the design?

a their age b their husband's name
c their favourite food

Find out about other interesting Hindu wedding traditions. Choose your favourite tradition and write a question for your partner to answer.

LEARN TO LEARN

Making connections

When you read an article, try to make connections with your own life and experiences. This can help you to relate to the people or places in the article and understand the article more easily.

6 **Think about a special celebration in your life and answer the questions.**

1 Is there a part of this article that reminds you of that special celebration?

2 Who and what does it remind you of: people, food, clothes, traditions?

7 COLLABORATE **Explain your connections to your partner. Are your partner's connections the same or different?**

Mini culture project p132

5 REVIEW

VOCABULARY

1 Complete the names of clothes with the missing vowels.

1 j _ _ ns
2 tr _ _ n _ rs
3 sh _ rt
4 b _ _ ts
5 h _ _ d _ _
6 sh _ rts
7 c _ p
8 j _ gg _ rs

2 Write the accessories.

1 two things you can wear on your wrist
2 two things you can put your money in
3 something you can use when it's raining
4 things you can wear in your ears
5 things you can wear on your hands when it's cold

3 Look at the pictures. What are they wearing? Write the clothes and accessories.

GRAMMAR

4 Complete the conversations. Use the correct form of the present continuous.

1 you / watch / TV just now?
✗ do / my homework
2 Lidia / wear / a red T-shirt today?
✗ wear / a blue shirt
3 Mike / chat / with his friends at the moment?
✗ take / a photo
4 your friends / listen / to music right now?
✗ play / video games

5 Complete the posts with the present simple or continuous form of the verbs.

What [1]… you usually … (wear) at school? I usually [2]… (wear) jeans and a T-shirt. It [3]… (rain) today so I [4]… (wear) a hoodie and I [5]… (carry) an umbrella!

[6]… your brother … (work) this afternoon?

No, he [7]… (not work) on Saturdays. He often [8]… (play) football, but today he [9]… (not do) that. He and Martin [10]… (shop) at the market.

Vocabulary

Clothes

boots
cap
flip-flops
hoodie
jacket
jeans
joggers
shirt
shorts
skirt
T-shirt
trainers

Accessories

belt
bracelet
earrings
gloves
necklace
purse
ring
scarf
sunglasses
umbrella
wallet
watch

Grammar

Present continuous
Present continuous and present simple

5 FINISHED?

1 Write the names of the clothes. Then make a crossword with the words.

2 What accessories do you need today? Complete the words with the missing vowels.

3 Look at the picture. Use the words in the table to make six sentences with the present continuous. Use all the verbs.

Danny	eat	to music.
	wear	to school.
Kate	carry	an apple.
	walk	watches.
Danny and Kate	not listen	a guitar.
	not wear	a jacket.

4 Compare the pictures of Aya. Write four sentences about her usual routine and the things she's doing today.

She usually wears a T-shirt, but this morning …

6 SPORT FOR LIFE

LEARNING OUTCOMES

I can ...

- understand texts about sport
- book tickets
- write a profile
- understand how to use comparatives and superlatives
- talk about sports
- say collocations out loud and remember vocabulary sets together
- make an information leaflet.

WATCH VIDEO 6.1

- Before you watch, guess three sports from the video.
- Watch and check. Which other sports can you see?
- Which sport do you want to try? Why?

KICK-OFF! 6.1

p75

GRAMMAR IN ACTION 6.2

p77

GRAMMAR IN ACTION 6.3

p78

EVERYDAY ENGLISH 6.4

VOCABULARY
Sports

1 (6.01) Match the words in the box with the photos. Then listen, check and repeat.

athletics basketball
(mountain/rock) climbing
gymnastics hockey rugby running
sailing swimming ~~table tennis~~
volleyball windsurfing yoga

a *table tennis*

2 (6.02) Listen. Which six sports do you hear?

LEARN TO LEARN

Saying collocations out loud

It's a good idea to learn words that go together, for example verbs and nouns. There are three main verbs we use with sports.

play ball sports
go sports that end in *-ing*
do other sports

When you learn new vocabulary, say the words out loud. This helps you remember them.

3 Write the sports from Exercise 1 in the spidergram. Say them out loud as you write them. How many more sports can you add?

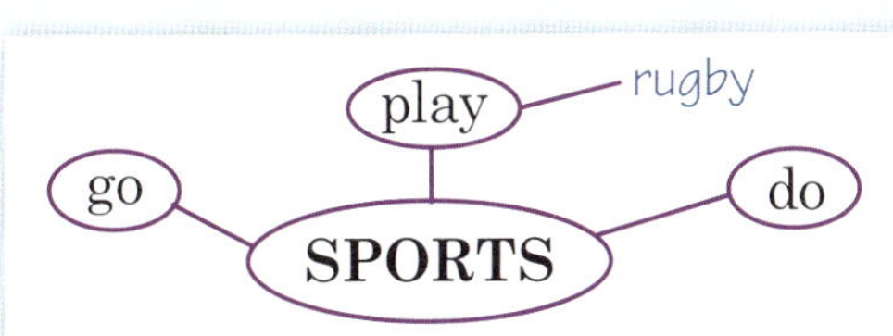

4 COLLABORATE Work in pairs. Test a partner. Say a sport out loud and your partner says the verb.

5 Think of another way to group sports and draw a spidergram. Tell your partner your sports. Can they guess the group?

6 **Use it!** Discuss the questions.

1 Which sports do you do? How often do you do them?
2 Do you prefer team sports or individual sports? Why?
3 Which sports do you want to try?

Explore it!

Guess the correct answer.

Tennis star Serena Williams wears … every day during a tennis tournament.

a a lucky necklace b different trainers
c the same socks

Find an interesting fact about a sport and write a question for your partner to answer.

READING

Online FAQs

1 What do you think the people in the photo are doing? Tell your partner.

6.03 2 Read and listen to the article. Match the questions with the answers in the FAQs.

Q1 – A5

3 Read the article again. Are the sentences *T* (true) or *F* (false)?

1 A bossaball team has a maximum of five people. T
2 Players can't use their feet.
3 A bossaball ball is the same size as a football.
4 You can play bossaball when it's raining.
5 The inventor of bossaball isn't a DJ.

4 Find the meaning of the words in **bold** in the online FAQs. Are they positive or negative? Can you add any more adjectives?

Positive	Negative
amazing	

5 Voice it! Discuss the questions.

1 Can you play bossaball in your town or city?
2 Do you think bossaball looks interesting or boring? Why?
3 Do you want to try it?

Bossaball

Do you need some help? You can't decide? What do you play: volleyball or football or maybe gymnastics? Don't worry! We've got the answer – you can do all of them. Bossaball is the answer!

FAQs

Q1: What is it?
Q2: Is it a team game?
Q3: Where can I play it?
Q4: How big is a bossaball?
Q5: Can players touch the ball?
Q6: Is there an age limit?

Answers

A1: It's almost the same size as a volleyball and smaller than a football.
A2: No, there isn't. It's suitable for people of all ages.
A3: Yes, it is. There are two teams and each team has three, four or five players.
A4: Yes, they can. Players can use their hands and arms or their feet.
A5: It's a mixture of football, volleyball and gymnastics with music. It's more **entertaining** than other ball sports and in some places it's becoming more **popular** than beach volleyball.
A6: You can play it indoors if the weather's **bad**, but people usually play outdoors in a park or on a beach.

Bossaball players think it's better than volleyball and it's more **exciting** than football. It definitely isn't **boring** to watch and it's even more **amazing** to play. What are you waiting for?

The inventor of Bossaball is Filip Eyckmans – he's Belgian. His favourite sports are tennis and football and he also loves music and dance. In fact, he's a DJ. Bossaball is a combination of his favourite things and it's great fun!

Finished? p83

GRAMMAR IN ACTION

Comparatives

Watch video 6.2
Which sports does he talk about?
Which sport is healthy?

Comparative adjectives		
Short adjectives	**Long adjectives**	**Irregular adjectives**
A bossaball is **smaller** than a football.	It's **more exciting** than football.	It's **better** than volleyball.
A football is **bigger** than a bossaball.	Bossaball is **more popular than** other sports.	The weather is **worse** today than yesterday.

Grammar reference p127   Pronunciation p143

1 **Write the comparative of the adjectives in the box.**

bad   big   boring
fast   good   tall

bad – worse

2 **Complete the sentences with the comparative form of the adjectives. Check your answers in the article on page 74.**

big   ~~entertaining~~
exciting   good   popular

1 Bossaball is … other ball sports.
   Bossaball is more entertaining than other ball sports.
2 Bossaball is … football.
3 A football is … a bossaball or a volleyball.
4 Bossaball is becoming … beach volleyball.
5 Do you think bossaball is … other sports you know?

3 **Write sentences with the comparative form of the adjectives. Use the correct form of the verb *be*.**

1 windsurfing (exciting) swimming
   Windsurfing is more exciting than sailing.
2 table tennis (interesting) yoga
3 climbing (difficult) volleyball
4 basketball players (tall) football players

4 COLLABORATE **Discuss the sentences in Exercise 3 with a partner. Do you agree? Find another pair with at least three answers the same as yours.**

Windsurfing is more exciting than sailing. Do you agree with that?

Yes, I agree. What about you?

5 **Use it!** **Write sentences to compare some of the things/ people below or use your own ideas. Use adjectives from the box or think of your own. Discuss with a partner. Do you agree?**

boring   comfortable   difficult   easy   exciting
good   healthy   interesting   smart   tasty

table tennis / tennis
hanging out with friends / going shopping
Italian food / Indian food
joggers / jeans

I think table tennis is more interesting than tennis. What do you think?

I don't agree. I think tennis is more interesting.

Finished? p83

1 throw / dive / pass

2 kick / hit / jump

3 catch / lift / bounce

4 climb / run / score

VOCABULARY AND LISTENING

Sports verbs

6.06 **1** **Choose the correct verb to describe the photos. Then listen, repeat and check. Can you guess the meaning of the other verbs?**

Get it right!

You **win** or **lose** a game, match, race or competition.

When you win, you **beat** the person or people you are competing with.

I want to win the race. **NOT** ~~I want to beat the race.~~

I think we can beat this team. **NOT** ~~I think we can win this team.~~

6.07 **2** **Choose the correct verbs. Can you guess the sports? Listen and check.**

This is a popular team sport in Asia. It's a combination of volleyball and football. Players can't use their hands. One player [1]*dives / passes* the ball to another player to start. Players [2]*run / kick* the ball with their feet. The first team to [3]*throw / score* 21 points in two games wins.

1 capoeira 2 underwater hockey 3 sepak takraw

This is a team game with six soft balls. It's popular in PE classes in the UK. Players [4]*lift / run* fast to pick up balls from the middle of the court. Then they [5]*dive / throw* their balls at the other team. If a ball [6]*hits / jumps* someone, that person is 'out'. Players can [7]*catch / score* a ball in their hands, but if it [8]*climbs / bounces* off another player, they can't use it.

1 basketball 2 dodgeball 3 volleyball

LEARN TO LEARN

Remembering vocabulary sets

Think about which verbs you can use for each sport. This will help you to remember the language you need to talk about sport.

3 COLLABORATE **Work with a partner and add other verbs to the diagram. Compare with another pair.**

basketball
bounce

4 Use it! **Choose a sport and describe it in three sentences. Use verbs from Exercise 1. Can your partner guess the sport?**

A conversation

6.08 **5** **Look at the photos. Why do you think these people are famous? Listen and check.**

Johanna Quaas

Sun Ming Ming

6.08 **6** **Listen again. Choose the correct answers.**

1 Johanna Quaas trains for a hour every … .
 a week b day c morning
2 She doesn't eat much … .
 a meat b fruit c meat or fruit
3 Sun Ming Ming's trainers are size … .
 a 41 b 55 c 37
4 Sun Ming Ming and his wife are both very … .
 a popular b tall c old

7 Voice it! **Discuss the questions.**

1 Who is the oldest person you know? Who is the tallest person?
2 Imagine you can interview Johanna Quaas or Sun Ming Ming. What do you want to ask?

GRAMMAR IN ACTION

Superlatives

Watch video 6.3
Who is the most amazing painter? Who can play the piano?

Superlative adjectives		
Short adjectives	**Long adjectives**	**Irregular adjectives**
Has Sun Ming Ming got the **biggest** feet in the world?	The article is about some of the **most amazing** sportspeople in the world.	Fruit and vegetables are the **best** things to eat.

Grammar reference p127

1 **Complete the sentences with the superlative form of the adjectives.**

1 Johnna Quaas is *the oldest* active gymnast in the world. (old)
2 She's probably … and … person in their 90s in the world. (fit; healthy)
3 Sun Ming Ming is … basketball player in the world. (tall)
4 Does the article say Sun Ming Ming is … player in his team? (good)

2 **Complete the sports quiz with the superlative form of the adjectives. Then predict the correct answers. Discuss with a partner.**

THE … (BIG) SPORTS QUIZ IN THE WORLD!

1 Fauja Singh is over 100 and he's very active. He's *the oldest* (old) person to *run a marathon* / *climb Mount Everest*.

2 Juju Noda hasn't got a car but she can drive. She is … (young) person to drive an *F4* / *F1* racing car.

3 Many people say that *basketball* / *football* is … (easy) sport to learn to play.

4 … (fast) time for the men's 100 m race at an Olympic Games is *9.58* / *9 seconds*.

5 *Volleyball* / *Table tennis* is … (popular) indoor sport. People of all ages play it. You only need a net, a ball and a bat.

6 … (good) food to eat before you do sport or exercise is a *carrot* / *banana*.

3 6.09 **Listen and check your answers to Exercise 2.**

4 **Use it!** **Write four sentences with your opinions about sports. Use the words in boxes A and B or choose your own. Then compare with a partner. Do you agree?**

A
easiest most boring
most difficult
most interesting on TV

B
do earn play watch

5 **Write sentences with superlative adjectives about the topics in the box or choose your own topics. Then ask and answer. Do you agree with your partner's opinions?**

day of the week (good)
food (delicious)
sportsperson (amazing)
person (happy)

Which is the best day of the week?

I think Friday is the best day of the week because I always finish school early. What about you?

Finished? p83

THE PE PROJECT

An information leaflet

1 **Look quickly at the leaflet. What is its purpose?**

1 to give directions to a sports club
2 to give information about a sport
3 to give transport times

2 **Read the leaflet and make notes on the ideas in the box.**

What? When? Where? Who?
Equipment One of the rules One of the benefits

3 **Read the leaflet again. Are the sentences *T* (true) or *F* (false)**

1 You need some special equipment to play streetball. F
2 There are sometimes ten players in a game of streetball.
3 Teams meet together before they go the court.
4 You can't touch the ball with your hands in streetball.
5 Some sports are more expensive than streetball.

How to design a leaflet

4 **Read the tips about designing a leaflet. Which ones do you think are good pieces of advice?**

a Use serious colours, not bright ones.
b Use photos and a map.
c Make sure the people are not smiling in the photos.
d Include contact details.
e Choose a clear font (if you're using a computer) or write neatly.
f Put all the information you know about the sport in your leaflet.

6.11 **5** **Listen to the advice and check your answers to Exercise 4.**

STREETBALL

WHAT IS IT?

It's outdoor basketball in your local area.

WHERE AND WHEN?

We meet every Tuesday at 5.30 pm at the West Avenue basketball court. Come along and join us.

Find us here:

WHO?

Everyone is welcome! You don't need to belong to a team and you don't need special training.

EQUIPMENT

We've got a basketball and nets. Just bring yourself and your trainers!

Teams

- Players get into teams at the court. There can be different numbers of people in a team. A team can play with only two players but there are never more than five.

Rules

Different streetball games have different rules, but these are ours:

- Players can bounce, throw and catch the ball.
- When you score, your team gets one point.
- After you score, your team keeps the ball. You don't give the ball to the other team.

WHY NOT COME ALONG AND MAKE NEW FRIENDS? Any questions? Contact Greg at gregscott@jmail.com.

How to win

In our games, a team wins when they score 7 points. In other streetball games, you often need to score more points – 10 or 11, or even 21.

BENEFITS

- It's cheaper than lots of other sports. In fact, it's free!
- It's a great way to get fitter and healthier!
- The best streetball matches are faster and more exciting than normal basketball.
- It's great fun!

FACT

Bucharest is the unofficial streetball capital of the world! Every year more than 1,000 streetball players travel to the Romanian capital city and they play streetball in a special competition.

TASK

Make an information leaflet

PLAN

6 **Work with a group. Choose a street sport or another sport and find out information about it. Then complete the steps below.**

- Decide on the information you want to include.
- Decide and choose the photos and illustrations to include.
- Draw a rough plan of the layout of the leaflet.
- Make a first draft of your leaflet.
- Discuss how you can improve your first draft.

PRESENT

7 **Prepare your final leaflet and present it to the class. Don't forget to include the items in the** CHECKLIST**.**

CHECKLIST **Remember to include:**

- facts about your street sport.
- photos, illustrations and maps.
- the tips in *How to* design a leaflet.

CHECK

8 COLLABORATE **Look at your classmates' leaflets. Do they use the items in the** CHECKLIST**? Which street sport do you think is the most interesting? Which one do you want to try?**

6 REVIEW

VOCABULARY

1 **Complete the sentences with the sports in the box.**

mountain climbing rugby sailing table tennis volleyball windsurfing yoga

1 You need a net to play … and … .
2 … is a ball game that people always play outdoors.
3 People usually do … indoors.
4 You need to be on the water to go … or … .
5 … can be dangerous, so you need very good equipment.

2 **Choose the correct verbs.**

1 We're playing football so we can *kick* / *score* the ball.
2 That looks heavy. Can you *climb* / *lift* it?
3 I want to *run* / *dive* a marathon one day.
4 *Catch* / *Throw* me that ball, please.
5 How do you *jump* / *score* in hockey?
6 It's important to *pass* / *hit* the ball in rugby.

GRAMMAR

3 **Write the comparative form of the adjectives.**

1 bad
2 big
3 easy
4 exciting
5 good
6 interesting

4 **Look at the information and write sentences. Use comparative and superlative adjectives.**

	Jack's opinion		
	Table tennis 	Rugby 	Hockey 
easy	★★★★★	★★	★
exciting	★	★★★★	★★
good	★★	★★★★	★

1 table tennis / easy
2 rugby / easy / hockey
3 hockey / exciting / table tennis
4 table tennis / good / hockey
5 rugby / good

Vocabulary

Sports

athletics
basketball
(mountain/rock) climbing
gymnastics
hockey
rugby
running
sailing
swimming
table tennis
volleyball
windsurfing
yoga

Sports verbs

bounce
catch
climb
dive
hit
jump
kick
lift
pass
run
score
throw

Grammar

Comparatives
Superlatives

6 FINISHED?

1 Put the letters in order and write the sports.

-ING: 1 mcibl, 2 nurn, 3 wmism

-BALL: 4 tbkaes, 5 otfo, 6 levoyl

-ICS: 7 amtsyng, 8 hetlat

2 Look at the picture. What are the people doing? Write sentences with the verbs in the box.

catch climb hit kick score throw

Kyle is kicking the football.

3 Write sentences to compare some of the things and people below. Use adjectives from the box. Compare your ideas with a partner.

boring difficult easy old popular

1. English / maths
2. pizza / pasta
3. sailing / gymnastics
4. swimming / climbing
5. I / my best friend
6. football / basketball in our country

4 Use the table to find six adjectives. Then complete the questions with the superlative forms of the adjectives. Answer them for you.

1	2	3	4	5	6	7	8	9	10	11	12	13
A	B	C	D	E	F	G	H	I	J	K	L	M
N	O	P	Q	R	S	T	U	V	W	X	Y	Z

1

7	1	6	7	12
T	*A*	*S*	*T*	*Y*

2

8	1	3	3	12

3

2	2	5	9	1	7

4

7	1	12	12

5

9	1	7	5	5	5	6	7	9	1	7

6

5	11	3	5	1	6	9	9	5

1. What is … thing you own?
2. Who is … person in your class?
3. What is … food you eat?
4. Who is … person in your family?
5. What is … book you know?
6. What is … programme on TV?

UNIT REVIEW 4–6

FUNCTIONAL LANGUAGE

SPEAKING

Everyday English

UNIT 4

Enjoy!
Here you go.
No problem.
No worries!

UNIT 5

It's a bargain
It's perfect.
No, honestly.
You're in luck!

UNIT 6

Got them!
Look!
That's crazy!
What are we waiting for?
Why not?

Useful Language

UNIT 4

Can I have …?
Can I help you?
How much is that?
Is that everything?
I'd like a/an/some …
That's … , please.
What kind?
What's in the … ?

UNIT 5

Can I help you?
Can I see the … one, please?
Have you got it in a different (size/colour/style)?
I'm looking for …
It comes in …
What about this one / these?

UNIT 6

How much are tickets?
Let's book them.
Let's go.
Shall we go?
They're (£45).
What's the (quickest/best/cheapest) way to get there?

WRITING

Useful Language

UNIT 4

Writing a description

We use *and* to add similar information.
We use *but* to contrast different information
We use *or* when there is a choice (usually between two things).

UNIT 5

Talking about a photo

at the back
in the middle
on the left/right
next to (someone)

UNIT 6

Giving extra information

We use *also* and *too* to give extra information.
We use *also* after the verb *be*.
We use *also* before other verbs.
We use *too* at the end of a sentence.

VOCABULARY

1 **Choose the correct option.**

1 Fizzy drinks and … are sweet.
a eggs b chocolate

2 Apples and … are fruit.
a bananas b carrots

3 I put hot … on my cereal for breakfast.
a beans b milk

4 Boots and … are for our feet.
a flip-flops b joggers

5 Alba wears shorts and … to play volleyball.
a trainers b shoes

6 It's very cold and Vi is wearing a scarf and … .
a earrings b gloves

7 Liliana always wears … to play football.
a joggers b a skirt

8 You can't kick the ball in table tennis and …
a hockey b sailing

9 Basketball and rugby players are good at …
a catching b climbing

10 In yoga, people don't score. They don't win or … .
a beat b lose

GRAMMAR

2 Read the text and choose the correct option.

[1]... students from the UK [2]... our school today. [3]... a boy called David and a girl called Elizabeth in our class. Elizabeth [4]... shorts and [5]... T-shirt. She hasn't got a uniform. They [6]... us about things in their country. They like playing basketball. Elizabeth says she is [7]... than David, but David doesn't agree! We're playing after lunch (we're [8]... eggs and [9]... rice). I prefer playing football. Elizabeth says that football is the [10]... sport in the world! I think that football is the [11]... interesting sport ever! [12]... a better sport!

1 a Any	b Some	c An
2 a are visiting	b visits	c are visit
3 a There are	b There's	c Is there
4 a is wearing	b wears	c wearing
5 a an	b any	c a
6 a tell	b is telling	c are telling
7 a best	b better	c good
8 a having	b have	c has
9 a any	b some	c a
10 a more easy	b easier	c easiest
11 a most	b more	c less
12 a There isn't	b Are there	c There aren't

Take the challenge!

1 **Complete the spidergram with adjectives for describing food.**

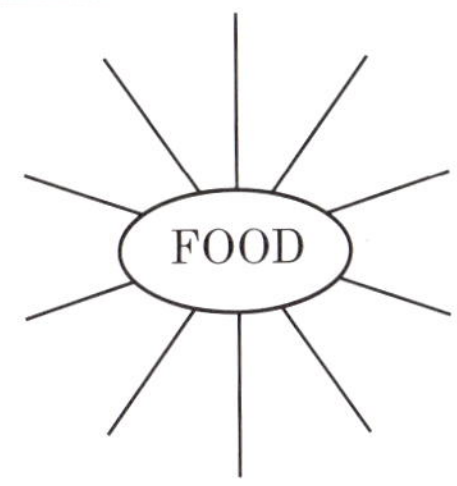

2 **Put the words in the correct place in the table. Look up any words you don't know.**

belt bracelet cap hoodie jumper leggings necklace purse skirt watch

Clothes	Accessories

3 **Complete the sentences with one word.**

1 Ali hasn't got ... beans on his plate.
2 There ... some milk in the fridge.
3 How ... bread have we got?

4 **Answer the questions with complete sentences.**

1 What are you wearing?
2 Are you doing sports this morning?
3 Which sports are more exciting than running?
4 Are there five questions in this exercise?

5 **Write a short paragraph about the clothes you like wearing or the sports you like playing.**

6 COLLABORATE **Swap your paragraph with a partner. Do you agree with their ideas?**

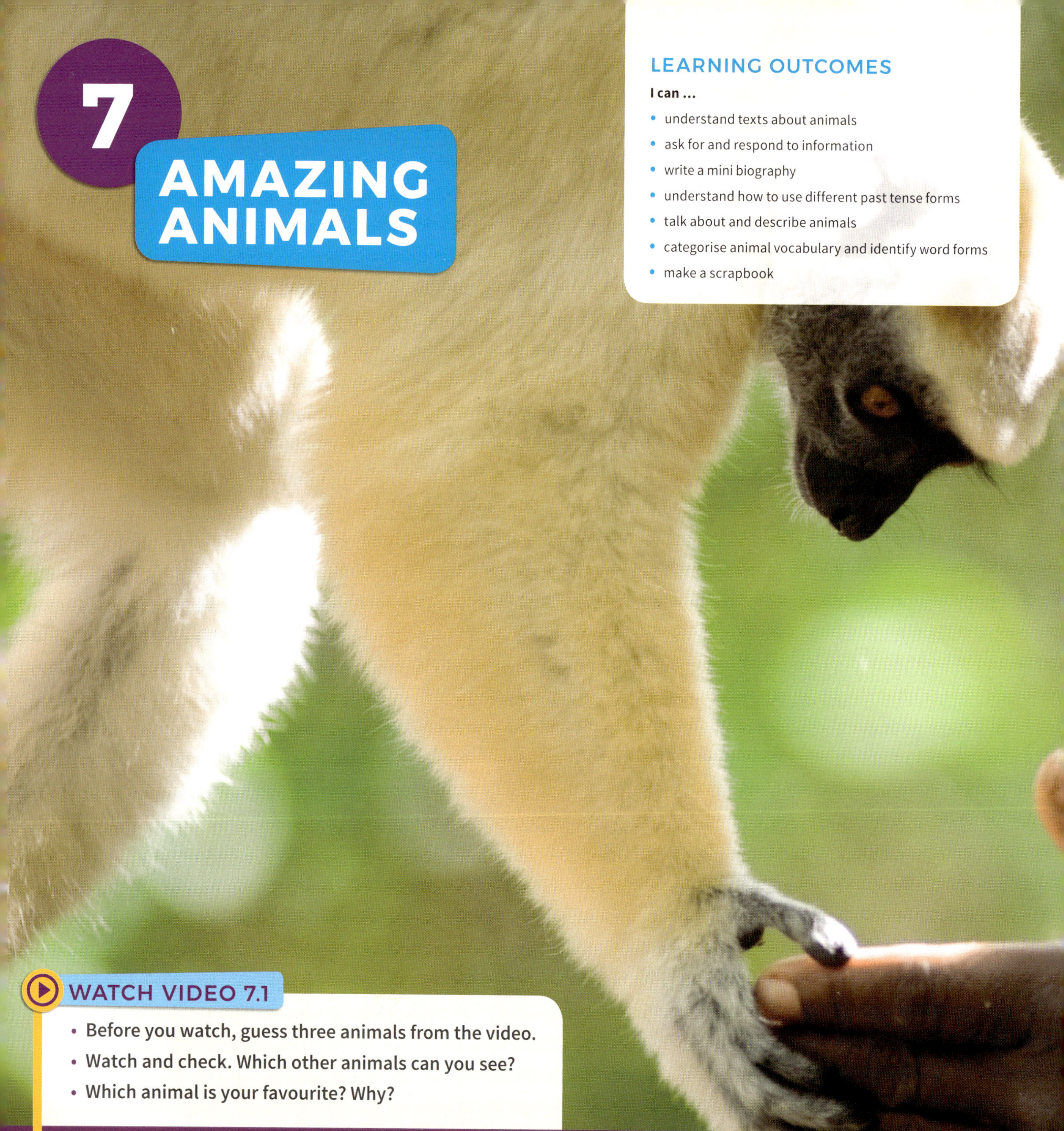

7 AMAZING ANIMALS

LEARNING OUTCOMES

I can ...

- understand texts about animals
- ask for and respond to information
- write a mini biography
- understand how to use different past tense forms
- talk about and describe animals
- categorise animal vocabulary and identify word forms
- make a scrapbook

WATCH VIDEO 7.1

- Before you watch, guess three animals from the video.
- Watch and check. Which other animals can you see?
- Which animal is your favourite? Why?

KICK-OFF! 7.1

p89

GRAMMAR IN ACTION 7.2

p91

GRAMMAR IN ACTION 7.3

p92

EVERYDAY ENGLISH 7.4

p94

GLOBETROTTERS 7.5

VOCABULARY

Animals

7.01 **1** Match ten of the animals in the box with the photos. Then listen, check and repeat. Which animals are not in the photos?

bear	crocodile	donkey	duck	
eagle	~~giraffe~~	hippo	horse	lion
monkey	mouse	parrot	snake	whale

a giraffe

7.02 **2** Listen to the noises. Write the animals you hear from Exercise 1.

LEARN TO LEARN

Word groups

When you learn new words, put them into groups. This helps you remember the meaning.

3 Complete the word groups with animals from Exercise 1. Then think of two more animals for each group.

Herbivore — *giraffe*
Omnivore — *bear*
Carnivore — *lion*

4 COLLABORATE Guess the extra animals in your partner's word groups.

5 **Use it!** Write new word groups for the animals. Tell your partner the animals but not the groups. Can they guess the group?

Category 1: mouse, parrot, snake

Is your group 'pets'?

Explore it!

Guess the correct answer.

A blue whale's tongue is as heavy as …

a a crocodile. **b** an elephant. **c** a giraffe.

Find an interesting animal fact. Then write a question for your partner to answer.

READING

Fact files

1 Tell your partner two things you know about gorillas, elephants and tigers.

2 Look at the photos. What is unusual about Snowflake, Nómade and Artico?

7.03 3 Read and listen to the fact files. Check your answers to Exercise 2 and find out two more things about each of the animals.

4 Choose the correct answer.

Which animals …

elephants tigers gorillas

1 build nests? *gorillas*
2 can hear with their feet?
3 are carnivores?
4 live in Southeast Asia?
5 are the heaviest?
6 live in African forests and mountains?

5 Find words in the fact files for the headings below. Think of two more words for each heading.

Animals: *gorilla*

Things animals eat:

Habitats:

6 Voice it! Discuss the questions.

1 Why do you think tigers have stripes?
2 Why do you think gorillas build a nest every night?
3 Why do you think some elephants are born without tusks?

Animals with a difference

Snowflake

From 1964 until 2003, there was a special gorilla in Barcelona Zoo. His name was Snowflake, and he was born in Africa. Snowflake was a celebrity in the zoo. He wasn't the same as the other gorillas because he was white. He was the world's only white gorilla.

WEIGHT Up to 270 kg
HABITAT African forests and mountains
FOOD Fruit, leaves and plants
FACT Gorillas are the largest mammals to build nests. They make a new nest every night!

Nómade

In the 1990s, in Mozambique, southern Africa, a baby elephant was born without tusks. Her name was Nómade. Her 11 sisters were born without them, too. In the 1930s, there weren't many African elephants without tusks, only 1%. But, in some areas of Africa today, 98% of female elephants are born like this.

WEIGHT Up to 6,000 kg
HABITAT African savannah and forests
FOOD Grass, leaves, trees, fruit and plants
FACT Elephants use their feet to listen.

Artico

In 2004, a Bengal tiger called Artico was born in a wildlife centre in Alicante, Spain. Artico wasn't like his parents. He was white with no stripes, but his parents weren't. They were orange with black stripes. Today, there are only about 20 Bengal tigers without stripes in the world.

WEIGHT Up to 230 kg
HABITAT Forests and mountains in Southeast Asia
FOOD Deer, buffalo, antelopes and other animals
FACT There aren't two tigers with the same stripes!

Finished? p97

Watch video 7.2
How many animals were there? What colour was the baby flamingo?

GRAMMAR IN ACTION

Was/were, there was/were

	Singular	Plural
+	His name **was** Snowflake.	They **were** orange with black stripes.
	There was a special gorilla.	There **were** many African elephants.
–	Artico **wasn't** like his parents.	His parents **weren't** white.
	There wasn't a white elephant.	**There weren't** any black tigers.
?	**Was** Artico white? Yes, he **was**. / No, he **wasn't**.	**Were** they tigers? Yes, they **were**. / No, they **weren't**.
	Was there a gorilla? Yes, **there was**. / No, **there wasn't**.	**Were there** any elephants? Yes, **there were**. / No, **there weren't**.

Grammar reference p125

1 **Find information in the fact files to correct the sentences.**

1 Snowflake and Artico were black.
They weren't black. They were white.
2 Snowflake was from Barcelona.
3 Nómade was born in Spain.
4 Nómade was an Indian elephant.
5 Artico was a lion.

2 **Remember the information from the fact files. Write sentences with *there was(n't)* and *there were(n't)*.**

There was a special gorilla in Barcelona until 2003.

3 COLLABORATE **Swap your sentences with a partner. Check your partner's sentences with the text. Are they correct?**

4 **Complete the text with *was(n't)/were(n't)* or *there was(n't)/there weren't*.**

50,000 years ago on the Indonesian island of Flores, [1]*there were* animals like elephants. But [2]... one difference: they [3]... very small. [4]... also Komodo dragons and huge rats on the island. [5]... people on Flores? Yes, [6]... but they [7]... like modern humans. They [8]... only about one metre tall. That's the size of a three year old! And their brain [9]... the size of an orange!

5 Use it! **Write questions with *was/were*. Then ask and answer with a partner.**

1 Where / you born? *Where were you born?*
In Ankara. Where were you born?
2 What / your favourite subject at primary school?
3 What / your favourite animal / when / you / six?
4 What / your favourite film / when / you / eight?
5 Who / your best friend / when / you / nine?
6 Where / you / at six o'clock on Sunday evening?

Finished? p97

VOCABULARY AND LISTENING

Adjectives

1 7.04 **Choose words to describe photos 1–6. Then listen, check and repeat. Can you guess the meaning of the other adjectives?**

2 7.05 **Complete the sentences with adjectives from Exercise 1. Then listen, check and repeat.**

1 Lions run at 80 km per hour. They are very fast.
2 Hippos kill 2,900 people each year in Africa. They're … . Be careful!
3 The blue whale is very … . Other animals can hear it from 800 km away!
4 Giraffes are tall, but they're also … . They weigh up to 1,400 kg.
5 Koalas are … animals. They spend most of their day sleeping in trees.
6 Mice can sing but we can't hear them. They are very … animals.

3 Use it! **Think of three animals. Write two adjectives to describe each one. Tell a partner your adjectives. Can they guess the animal?**

It's quiet and tiny. *Is it a mouse?*

A podcast

4 **Discuss the questions with a partner.**

1 What can parrots do?
2 Are parrots good pets? Why / Why not?

5 7.06 **Look at the photos. What do you think the podcast is about, a, b or c? Listen and check.**

a A hungry parrot
b A dangerous parrot
c A clever parrot

LEARN TO LEARN

Preparing to listen

Thinking about the questions before you listen can help you hear the correct answers.

6 COLLABORATE **Work with a partner. Read the questions in Exercise 7 and find the question words.**

7 7.06 **Listen again and answer the questions.**

1 How old was Hannah?
2 Who was really noisy?
3 Who wasn't at home on the day of the story?
4 Why was Hannah's toast on the table?
5 Where was Meagan when Hannah ate the toast?

8 **Work in pairs. Who can remember the most information about the story?**

There was a parrot. *There was a girl called Hannah.*

GRAMMAR IN ACTION

Past simple: regular and irregular

Watch video 7.3
Where was the school trip?
How many bears were there?

	Regular verbs	Irregular verbs
+	They **lived** in Denver.	They **did** lots of things together.
–	She **didn't want** to wait.	Meagan **didn't have** any children.
Past time expressions	It **happened** more than ten years **ago**. You **shared** some great stories with us **last week**.	We **heard** this amazing story **yesterday**.

Grammar reference p125
Pronunciation p143

1 Complete the sentences. Then correct three of the facts about the listening.

Meagan …

1 and Samantha *studied* (study) in Denver.
2 … (not hear) Willie.
3 … (not make) Hannah some toast.
4 … (leave) the toast on the table.
5 … (see) Hannah's face was blue.
6 and Willie … (not save) Hannah's life.

7.10 **2** Complete the text. Then listen and check.

Gilberto 'Chito' Shedden was a fisherman from Costa Rica. One day, he [1]*saw* (see) a crocodile in the river. It [2]… (have) an eye problem, so Chito [3]… (decide) to take the crocodile home. He [4]… (feed) the crocodile and [5]… (give) it medicine. He called it Pocho. Chito [6]… (not leave) Pocho and at night they [7]… (sleep) in the same room. When Pocho was healthy again, Chito [8]… (take) him to the river. But Pocho [9]… (not want) to stay in the river, so he [10]… (follow) Chito home! Pocho and Chito [11]… (become) best friends until Pocho [12]… (die) a few years ago.

3 **Use it!** Write five true or false sentences about you. Use the past simple (see p144) and the past words below.

yesterday ago
last week/month/year/summer/Friday

I went to Brazil on holiday three weeks ago.

4 Take turns to say your sentences. Can your partner guess which are true and false?

Finished? p97

8 LOST AND FOUND

LEARNING OUTCOMES

I can ...

- understand texts about an unusual town and finding treasure
- help a friend
- write a blog post
- understand how to ask past simple questions
- talk about places in a city and personal possessions
- use compound nouns and photos to predict content
- do an interview.

WATCH VIDEO 8.1

- Before you watch, where do you look when you lose something?
- Watch and check. What do archaeologists do?
- What is your favourite treasure? Why?

KICK-OFF! 8.1

p101

GRAMMAR IN ACTION 8.2

p103

GRAMMAR IN ACTION 8.3

p104

EVERYDAY ENGLISH 8.4

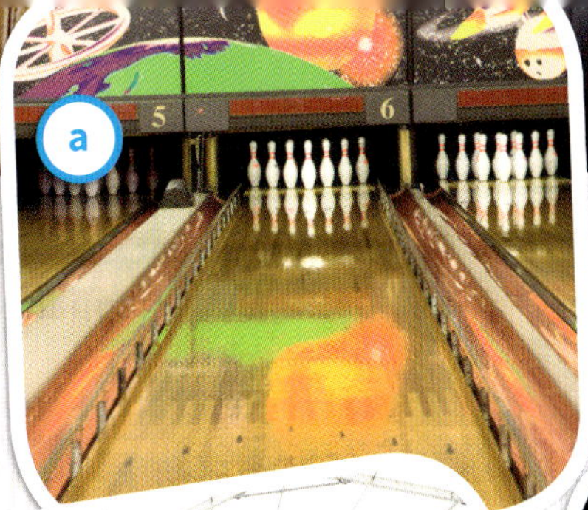

VOCABULARY
Places in town

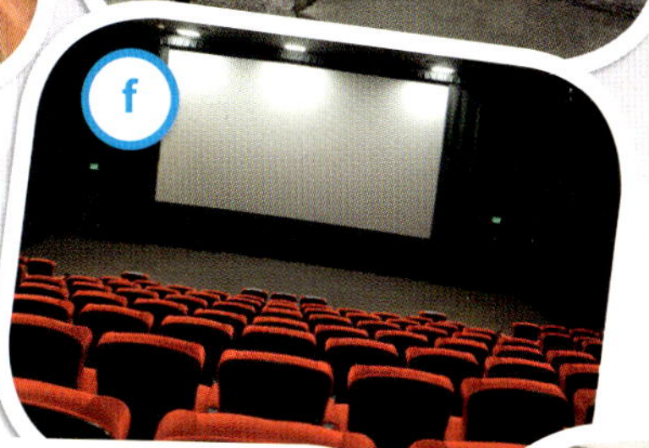

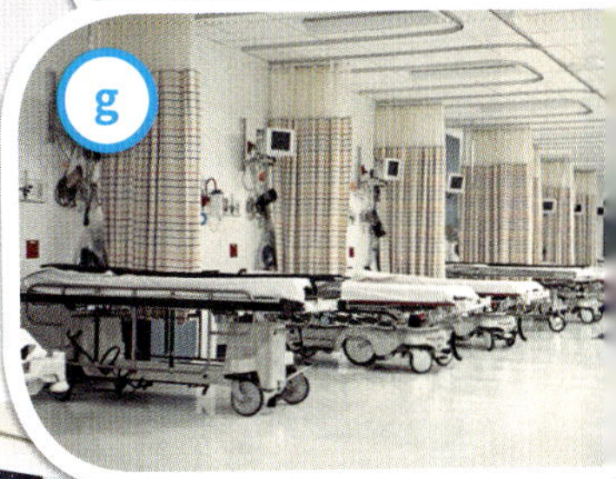

8.01 **1** **Match the places in the box with the photos. Then listen, check and repeat.**

aquarium ~~bowling alley~~ car park cinema hospital ice rink post office shopping centre skate park sports centre swimming pool

a *bowling alley*

2 **Which places in Exercise 1 are in your town? Which ones do you sometimes or often go to? Compare with a partner.**

LEARN TO LEARN

Compound nouns

There are lots of compound nouns in English. The two words together usually have a different meaning from the separate words. When you learn them together, you learn new vocabulary!

3 **Look at the places in Exercise 1. Which words are compound nouns?**

4 COLLABORATE **Work with a partner. Your partner says the first part of a compound noun and you say the second part. Can you think of any more compound nouns?**

5 **Use it!** **Answer the questions. Then write three more questions about the places in Exercise 1 for your partner to answer.**

Where do you go to …

1 buy clothes and accessories?
2 see fish and sea creatures?
3 see a doctor?
4 watch a film?
5 do sports and exercise?

Explore it!

Guess the correct answer.

The Dubai Mall is one of the largest shopping centres in the world. There are 1,200 shops and there's also …

a an aquarium b a swimming pool c a skate park

Find another interesting fact about the Dubai Mall. Then write a question for your partner to answer.

VOCABULARY AND LISTENING

Personal possessions

8.07 **1** **Match the words with the photos. Listen, check and repeat.**

bus pass camera ~~concert ticket~~ headphones ID card keys laptop money passport phone portable charger tablet

1 *concert ticket*

2 **Look in your schoolbag. How many of the possessions in Exercise 1 have you got?**

3 Use it! **Describe a possession you used yesterday. Can your partner guess?**

I used this on the bus yesterday.

Your phone?

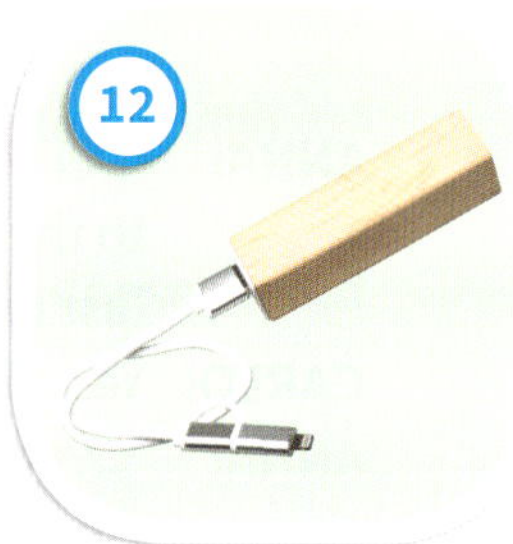

A radio interview

LEARN TO LEARN

Using photos to predict content

Before you listen, look carefully at any pictures. Think about the connection between them. This can help you to understand what you are listening to better.

4 COLLABORATE **Look at the photos in Exercise 6 and read the sentences. Work with a partner and say what you think the story is about.**

8.08 **5** **Listen to the radio interview and check your answers to Exercise 4. Were you correct?**

8.08 **6** **Listen again. Are the sentences *T* (true) or *F* (false)?**

1. Andres goes out every weekend to look for treasure. F
2. Andres uses special equipment when he does his hobby.
3. Detectorists always collect old drinks cans.
4. Andres and his dad are members of a club.
5. When detectorists find treasure, they dance.
6. Andres found some very old Roman money.

7 Voice it! **Discuss the questions.**

1. Do you know anyone with an unusual hobby like Andres?
2. Imagine you find some ancient treasure. How do you feel? What do you do?

GRAMMAR IN ACTION

Past simple: *Wh-* questions

Watch video 8.3
What did Nick lose?
Where did Nick find them?

Where	did	you	go last weekend?
Who		you	go with?
What		your dad	do?
When		you	take that photo?
How		Andres	find the treasure?

Grammar reference p126

1 **Put the words in the correct order to write the questions. Then match them with the answers.**

1 Andres / find / did / the treasure / when?
   When did Andres find the treasure? b
2 did / Andres / find / where / the treasure?
3 Andres / how / feel / did?
4 he / what / did / do?
5 send the photos to / did / Andres's dad / who?

a Shocked.
b Last weekend.
c He shouted for his dad and did a dance.
d The local museum.
e In a field near his house.

8.09 **2** **Complete the conversations with the question words and the correct form of the verbs. Listen and check.**

A How much Where

A: Hey. Cool headphones! [1]*Where did* you *get* (get) them?
B: I bought them online.
A: [2]… they … (cost)?
B: €20.

B What Which Who

A: [3]… you … (do) on Saturday afternoon?
B: I went to the cinema.
A: [4]… you … (go) with?
B: I went with Lukas.
A: [5]… film … you … (see)?
B: We saw the new Avengers film. It was amazing!

C Where When

A: [6]… your dad … (lose) his passport?
B: He lost it yesterday.
A: [7]… he … (lose) it?
B: I don't know but I know he needs to find it because we're going to Paris tomorrow!

3 **Have a conversation like conversation B in Exercise 2. Substitute the information so it is true for you.**

4 **Use it!** **Think of your favourite possession. Then ask questions to guess your partner's possession. Use some of the questions below.**

when / get it? why / want it?
where / buy it? how / feel / when you got it?
how much / cost? when / last / use it?

When did you get it?

I got it for my 13th birthday.

Finished? p109

SPEAKING

Losing things

8.10 **1** Listen to the conversation. Where is Billy's bus pass?

BILLY:	I can't find my bus pass, Gemma.
GEMMA:	Don't panic!
BILLY:	I need it to get home.
GEMMA:	Calm down. Let's think. [1]… .
BILLY:	On the bus this morning.
GEMMA:	Right, OK. [2]… .
BILLY:	I can't remember.
GEMMA:	Well, [3]… .
BILLY:	Yes, I did. I'm certain.
GEMMA:	[4]… ?
BILLY:	Maybe.
GEMMA:	Right. What's that?
BILLY:	Yesterday's lunch.
GEMMA:	Gross! What's this?
BILLY:	My bus pass. I don't know what to say.
GEMMA:	Thanks, maybe?

8.10 **2** Complete the conversation with phrases from the *Useful language* box. Then listen again and check.

Useful language

Did you have it when you (got to school)?
Did you put it (in your bag)?
What did you do with it after that?
When did you last (have/use/see) it?

3 Look at the *Everyday English* box. How do you say these phrases in your language?

Watch video 8.4
Everyday English

Calm down. Don't panic!
Gross! Let's think.

4 Gemma uses some of the phrases in the *Everyday English* box to keep Billy calm. Can you think of any other phrases to do this?

TASK

Plan your own conversation

PLAN

5 Work with a partner. Think about what you lost, when you last had/used it, where you were, what you did with it. Use your own experience or your imagination.

SPEAK

6 Practise the conversation.

CHECKLIST **Remember to include:**

- past simple questions and answers
- the vocabulary from this unit
- the *Useful language* and *Everyday English* phrases.

CHECK

7 COLLABORATE **Work with another pair. Listen to their conversation and write examples of language they use from the** CHECKLIST**. What did they lose? Did they find it? If so, where?**

WRITING
A blog post

Tanya's *thoughts on life, the universe and the rest*

A bad day!

It started this morning. I didn't hear my alarm so I got up late. I didn't have time for breakfast and I couldn't find my bus pass so I ran all the way to school. It got worse!

My first class was maths – I forgot my book. Guess what? It didn't matter because we had a surprise test. It was really hard.

At lunchtime, I realised I didn't have any money so I didn't have any lunch. I went to the library instead. Bad news.

But the worst thing happened later. After school, I went to the skate park but I lost my mobile so I can't text, take any selfies or make calls. I'm using my brother's laptop to write this. Tragic.

Did you all have a good Friday? What did you do? Let me know.

Friday, June 26th posted at 9.30pm

Comments

1 **Read the blog post. Give one reason why Tanya had a bad day.**

2 **Read the blog post again. Put the events in Tanya's day in the correct order (1–5).**

a She didn't have any lunch.
b She didn't hear her alarm. 1
c She lost her mobile.
d She couldn't find her bus pass.
e She had a maths test.

Useful language

I didn't hear my alarm **so** I got up late.

3 **Look at the *Useful language* box and find more examples of *so* in the blog post.**

4 **Join the sentences with *so*.**

1 I was late. I ran. I was late so I ran.
2 The students had a test. They revised.
3 We didn't have any money. We didn't buy any concert tickets.
4 Emma wanted to apologise. She rang me.

TASK
Write your own blog post about a bad day

PLAN

5 **Before you write, think about the answers to these questions.**

When did the bad day start?
What problems did you have?
When did each problem happen?
What did you do?
How did you feel?

Remember to use this structure:

Title
1: When it started
2: At school
3: The middle of the day
4: The end of the day
Sign off: Ask two questions.

WRITE

6 **Write your blog post.**

CHECKLIST **Remember to include:**

- a title
- four paragraphs
- *so* to join ideas and explain the results
- past simple questions at the end.

CHECK

7 COLLABORATE **Swap your blog post with a partner. Have they got the items in the CHECKLIST? Whose day was the worst?**

Finished? p109

THE HISTORY PROJECT

An interview

1 Look at the photos. What's the connection between them?

8.11 2 Listen to Ruby's and Jacob's interview. Check your answers to Exercise 1. Were you correct?

8.11 3 Listen again and answer the questions.

1. How many people were there in Clarissa's family? Ten
2. What was her life like when she was younger?
3. What buildings were in Clarissa's street?
4. What happened to Cookie?
5. In Clarissa's opinion, what are the most important things in life? Do you agree?

8.12 4 Listen to a teacher talking about questions for a good interview. What are the three types of questions?

8.11 5 Listen again to the interview. Are Ruby and Jacob's interview questions open, closed or follow-up?

6 Read the *How to …* box. Put the tips (a–h) in the groups in the table. Some tips can go in more than one group.

Before the interview	During the interview	After the interview
	a	

How to do a recorded interview

a Remember why you're doing the interview – always have the reason in your mind or on a piece of paper or post-it note.
b Don't take up too much of the interviewee's time.
c Use open and follow-up questions.
d Organise your questions before the interview.
e Say thank you at the beginning and at the end.
f Listen and make notes when appropriate.
g Send a thank you email / letter.
h Check your phone is working and take a portable charger or take a pen and some paper.

7 Do you think Ruby and Jacob followed all the tips?

LIVING MEMORIES

Radley Boulevard 1947

Radley Boulevard today

Cookie

Clarissa 1947

Clarissa today

TASK

Interview someone about their life in the past

PLAN

8 **Work in pairs. Choose the person to interview for the Living Memories project. Think about the things you want to know. Then complete the steps below and do the interview.**

Before the interview

- Plan and prepare your questions.
- Check how much time you have to do the interview.
- Check your equipment (phone or pen and paper).

During the interview

- Introduce yourself.
- Explain the purpose of the interview.
- Record the interview and make notes.
- Listen carefully to the answers.

After the interview

- Thank the person.
- Type or write up the interview.
- Send the person a copy and a thank you email / letter.

PRESENT

9 **Play your recording to the class or display your written interviews on the wall with the photos. Don't forget to include the items in the CHECKLIST.**

CHECKLIST **Remember to include:**

- polite language
- photos of the person and place in the past and now
- the tips in *How to* do a recorded interview.

CHECK

10 COLLABORATE **Listen to your classmates' interviews or read them. Do they use the items in the CHECKLIST? Did they do a good interview?**

Interview questions for Clarissa Briggs

Date and time: 17th June, 10.00 am

Place: 937 Houston Street East

1 Where did you live as a child?

2 What did you do each day?

3 Why did things change?

4 How did you feel about the change?

5 Who was Cookie?

6 What lessons for life did you learn from that experience?

8 REVIEW

VOCABULARY

1 **Match 1–6 with a–f to make places in a town.**

1 bowling
2 ice
3 post
4 shopping
5 skate
6 swimming

a park
b centre
c pool
d alley
e office
f rink

2 **Choose the correct words.**

1 Laura always wears her *laptop* / *headphones* when she listens to music.
2 I can't get the bus home. I didn't bring my *passport* / *bus pass*.
3 My *phone* / *concert ticket* isn't working. I can't send any texts.
4 We want to buy some sandwiches. Have you got any *keys* / *money*?
5 They're great photos. Did you use your new *camera* / *charger*?

GRAMMAR

3 **Write the past simple questions 1–5 and match them with the answers a–e.**

1 you / have / an egg for breakfast this morning?
2 you and Mike / go / shopping yesterday?
3 Teresa / send / you a text this morning?
4 your new passport / arrive / last week?
5 your parents / watch / the concert?

a No, but she rang me last night.
b Yes, it did.
c No, I always have toast.
d No, they didn't.
e Yes, we bought some clothes at the market.

4 **Look at the answers and write the questions. Use the question words in the box.**

How many | What | When | Where | Who

1 A: you / on TV last night?
B: We watched a really exciting film.
2 A: your cousin / her keys?
B: She lost them at the shopping centre.
3 A: Ana's grandparents / to Spain?
B: They came here in 1997.
4 A: Martin / at the cinema?
B: He met Jamie and Emma.
5 A: eggs / you?
B: I bought twelve.

Vocabulary

Places in a town

aquarium
bowling alley
car park
cinema
hospital
ice rink
post office
shopping centre
skate park
sports centre
swimming pool

Personal possessions

bus pass
camera
concert ticket
headphones
ID card
keys
laptop
money
passport
phone
portable charger
tablet

Grammar

Past simple: *Yes/No* and *Wh-* questions

8 FINISHED?

1 Look at the plan of Streetville. Correct the names of the places.

1 *aquarium*

2 Use all the words in the same colour to write five questions. Then answer them.

you	last weekend	Did	do any sport	Did
go bowling	Did	yesterday	Did	your parents
come into the room	you	Did	this morning	ten minutes ago
last night	use your mobile	your teacher	watch TV	you and your friends

3 Look at the pictures and complete the sentences. Compare your ideas with a partner.

1 Ellie didn't have much  so she couldn't buy a  .

2 When my  stopped working I used my  .

3 You can use your  or your  to show who you are.

4 Sam lost his  and his  on his way to school.

4 Use the words in the table to make a question for each picture.

What	did	I	spend	outside?
When		she	wear	this cheese?
Where		we	see	my glasses?
Why		he	buy	at the sports shop?
How much money		you	put	that outfit?

1

2

3

4

5

9 SUMMER FUN

LEARNING OUTCOMES

I can ...

- understand texts about an adventure weekend and holidays
- make suggestions and respond to them
- write an email
- understand how to use the future tenses
- talk about outdoor life and holidays
- make collocations and spidergrams and understand different types of English
- design a poster.

WATCH VIDEO 9.1

- Before you watch, what do people do on holiday?
- Watch and check. Where did Juno and Raúl go on holiday?
- Which holiday do you prefer? Juno or Raúl's? Why?

KICK-OFF! 9.1

p113

GRAMMAR IN ACTION 9.2

p115

GRAMMAR IN ACTION 9.3

p116

EVERYDAY ENGLISH 9.4

p118

GLOBETROTTERS 9.5

VOCABULARY

Outdoor life

a

b

c

d

e

f

g

h
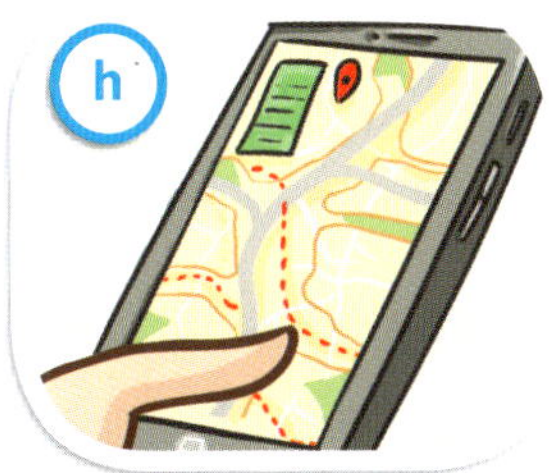

i

j

9.01 **1 Match the activities in the box with the pictures. Then listen, check and repeat.**

build a shelter   catch fish   collect wood   cook over a campfire   find food and water   identify plants   light a fire   ~~pick fruit~~   read a map   use a compass

a *pick fruit*

9.02 **2 Choose the correct expressions. Listen and check.**

1 A: I'm thirsty.
  B: OK. Let's *find some water.* / *light a fire.*
2 A: I'm hungry.
  B: Why don't we *build a shelter* / *pick some fruit?*
3 A: This plant looks delicious. Let's try it.
  B: No. It's always important to *collect wood* / *identify plants first.*
4 A: Oh no! We're lost. Can you *read a map* / *identify plants?*
  B: Of course, but we don't know where we are. Let's *cook over a campfire* / *use a compass.*

LEARN TO LEARN

Collocation

Some verbs and nouns go together in English. When you learn verbs, try to learn them in a phrase with a noun.

3 Look at the activitites in Exercise 1 again. Take turns to say a noun or a verb for your partner to complete the phrase. How many can you remember?

4 COLLABORATE Think of other nouns that go with the verbs in Exercise 1, for example, *collect magazines*. Make a list of them. Compare with a partner and add any new collocations to your lists.

5 Use it! Discuss the questions.

1 Which activities in Exercise 1 can you do?
2 Which ones do you think are the most useful? Why?
3 Which ones do you want to learn?

Explore it!

Guess the correct answer.

Mauro Prosperi ran a marathon in the Sahara Desert in 1994 but he got lost. How long did he survive without water?

a one day   b ten days   c three weeks

Find an interesting fact about people's amazing survival skills. Then write a question for your partner to answer.

READING

A leaflet

1 Look at the photos. What do you think the leaflet is about? What do you want to know about it?

9.03 2 Put the questions (a–d) in the right places in the leaflet (1–4). Then read and listen to check your answers.

a What will you eat?
b Who will look after you?
c Where will you sleep?
d What will you do during the weekend?

3 Guess the meaning of the words in **bold** in the leaflet.

4 Choose the correct answer. Which person …

You Adem Havva

1 will practise their wood skills? *You*
2 will learn new things?
3 will organise a cooking competition?
4 will build a shelter?
5 knows about wild food?
6 knows how to track animals?

5 Voice it! Discuss the questions.

1 What do you think is the most interesting part of WILD Weekend?
2 Why is it important …
to be careful when lighting a fire?
to identify plants before eating them?

WILD Weekend

Do you want a new adventure this summer? Join us at one of our WILD centres in Turkey. Every weekend from Friday to Sunday.

1 …
In a bed? In a tent? No, you'll sleep in a shelter. You'll build it yourself with **leaves** and **branches**.

2 …
You won't be near any shops or a supermarket so you'll find your own food. You'll learn to catch fish, collect fruit and identify plants to eat.

3 …
Daytimes
Why not try some of our amazing adventure activities?

- Go sea kayaking or diving in the sea.
- Go for a bike ride or go horse riding in the mountains.
- Learn to track animals or practise your wood skills.

Evenings

- Get to know your new friends and compare your WILD days.
- Sing, listen to ancient Turkish legends, cook potatoes over the campfire and relax.

4 …
Meet your instructors!

Hi! I'm Adem. I'm an **expert** in extreme survival. I'll teach you survival skills for life. You'll also learn how to **track** animals and how to work with wood. You'll learn new things about yourself and you'll begin to love outdoor life.

Hi! I'm Havva and I'll help you to find, prepare and cook your own food. You won't want to eat food from a supermarket ever again! Look out for my campfire cooking challenge! Will you be a winner?

Join us for a WILD Weekend You'll learn new skills, make new friends for life and have fun! Will you want to do it again? Of course, you will! For more information and booking details, visit our website now: http://wildweekend.org.globalnet

Finished? p121

GRAMMAR IN ACTION

Future with *will/won't*

Watch video 9.2
Where is he going? What will they do there?

	I/You/He/She/It/We/They
+	I'**ll teach** you survival skills.
	You'**ll sleep** in a shelter.
–	You **won't** be near any shops.
?	**Will** you be a winner?
	Yes, you will. / No, you **won't**.
	What **will** you **eat**?

Grammar reference p125

1 Complete the summary with *will* or *won't*. Check your answers in the leaflet on page 112.

WILD Weekend

What [1]will you do?

You [2]… sleep in your own bed.

You [3]… build a shelter and sleep outdoors.

You [4]… buy your food in shops or supermarkets.

You [5]… find and cook your own food.

You [6]… learn new skills for life.

[7]… you have fun? Yes, you [8]… .

2 Complete the TV advert below with the correct form of *will* and the verbs in the box.

choose get not have
not see ~~spend~~ survive work

9.04 **3** COLLABORATE Swap your answers with a partner. Listen and check your partner's work.

4 **Use it!** Imagine you are one of the people in *Teen Challenge*. Ask and answer questions about how you will survive on the island. Use the ideas below or your own ideas.

- miss your family and friends?
- survive without your mobile?
- learn new skills?

TEEN CHALLENGE!

A group of five young teenagers [1]will spend three nights alone on an island.

In tonight's programme the group [2]… important information about the challenge and they [3]… five items to take with them.

For three nights, these young teenagers:

- [4]… their family or friends
- [5]… phones or laptops
- [6]… together to find shelter, food and water.

[7]… they … the toughest three days of their lives?

Watch tonight and find out!

Finished? p121

VOCABULARY AND LISTENING

Holidays

9.05 **1** Match the words with the photos. Listen, check and repeat.

apartment B&B (bed & breakfast) camper van caravan chalet cottage hotel tent ~~youth hostel~~

1 *youth hostel*

2 Which two types of accommodation do you think are best for each of these holidays?

1 a cheap beach holiday
2 a skiing holiday
3 a comfortable city holiday
4 a driving tour across the country

LEARN TO LEARN

Personalising spidergrams

It's a good idea to personalise a spidergram with colours or symbols and illustrations of your own to help you remember vocabulary more easily.

3 COLLABORATE Make a spidergram with words from Exercises 1 and 2. How many more can you add? Swap your spidergram with another pair.

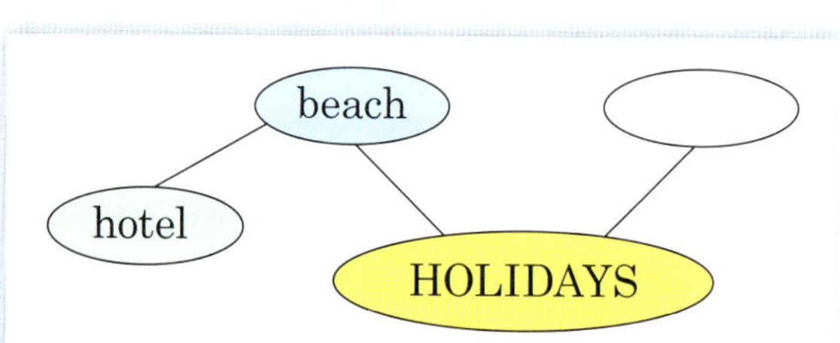

4 Use it! Choose your ideal type of holiday and a place to stay. Compare with a partner.

My ideal holiday is a skiing holiday and I want to stay in a chalet.

A conversation

9.06 **5** Listen. What are Matteo and Libby talking about?

9.06 **6** Listen again. Write *M* (Matteo) or *L* (Libby).

Who …

1 doesn't want to stay in a village
2 has got a younger brother and sister
3 talks about the tallest building in the world
4 can ski on holiday?

9.06 **7** Copy and complete the table with the correct information about the people's holiday trips. Listen again and check.

	Matteo and his parents	Libby and her parents
1 Type of accommodation		
2 Start of holiday trip		
3 Length of holiday trip		
4 Destination(s)		

8 Voice it! Discuss the questions.

1 What is your dream holiday?
2 What types of holiday and holiday accommodation are popular in your country?

GRAMMAR IN ACTION

Present continuous for future

Watch video 9.3
Where is the school band going? What are they going to do there?

	Present continuous: to talk about fixed arrangements in the future
+	I'**m going to** a football camp for two weeks in June.
+	They'**re working** in July.
–	She **isn't staying** in a chalet.
?	**Are they working** in July? **Yes**, **they are**. / **No**, **they aren't**.
?	Where **are** you **staying**? What **are** you **doing** in July?

Grammar reference p125

1 Write questions with the present continuous. Then match them with the correct answers.

1 where / Matteo / spend / July?
Where is Matteo spending July? f
2 what / Matteo's parents / do / on 1st August?
3 Matteo / travel / on his own?
4 where / Libby / go / on holiday?
5 when / she / leave?

a No, he isn't. He's travelling with his family.
b She's going to Dubai.
c She's leaving on 29th July.
d They're hiring a camper van.
e He's spending it in his grandma's village.

2 Look at your diary. Write sentences about your arrangements this week.

3 Swap your sentences with a partner. Tell another pair what your partner's plans are this week.

Be going to

	be going to: to talk about future intentions
+	We're going to visit a waterpark.
–	Matteo isn't going to travel in France.
?	Are you going to go on holiday this summer?
?	What are you going to do there?

Grammar reference p125 Pronunciation p143

4 Write questions with *going to*. Then ask and answer.

1 Matteo and Libby / stay at home / this summer?
Are Matteo and Libby going to stay at home this summer? No, they aren't.
2 who / swim / in six different swimming pools?
3 Libby / go up / the tallest building in the world?
4 what / Matteo / do / in each city?

5 Look at Jared and Wasim's intentions for this summer. Write sentences with *going to*.

1 *Jared is going to learn to make pizza. Wasim …*

Summer intentions	Jared	Wasim
1 learn to make pizza	✓	✗
2 sleep in a tent	✗	✓
3 study in the library	✗	✗
4 get lots of exercise	✓	✓

6 **Use it!** Ask and answer questions about your arrangements and intentions this summer.

What are you doing this summer? *I'm …*

7 Tell the rest of the class about your partner.
Alex is going to an adventure camp this summer.

Finished? p121

AROUND THE WORLD

READING

A webpage

1 Choose the answer you think is correct.

1 More than … American children and teenagers are going to a summer camp this year.

a 9 million b 11 million

2 The first American summer camp opened … years ago.

a 50 b 150

9.10 **2 Read and listen to the webpage and check your answers to Exercise 1. Write two more things you would like to know about American summer camps.**

3 Read the webpage again. Match the sentences with the camps.

1 You will work with professional coaches.
2 It lasts for three weeks.
3 You will spend a month on this camp.
4 This camp lasts for two weeks.
5 You won't hear any English while you are on this camp.
6 You can only do this course if you are not a beginner.

Globetrotters

Watch video 9.5
A summer camp in …

- How long is the camp in Costa Rica?
- Which animals will you see?
- Which animal will you protect?

Explore it!

True or False?

In the state of Georgia, it's illegal to live on a boat for more than 30 days.

Find out another interesting or unusual law about an American state and write a question for your partner to answer.

Your Guide to American Summer Camps

What are you going to do in the summer vacation? Here in the USA, more than 11 million children and teenagers are going to summer camps. The first summer camp opened more than 150 years ago and there are now more than 1,200 summer camps to choose from.

Here are our four favorite camps this week.

Tech Camp, Massachusetts

You'll be in a great university in the state, at the heart of technology! In just three weeks, you'll learn to build robots with our older students. They'll help you to develop useful skills like game and web design. You'll stay in an apartment on our beautiful campus and experience college life.

4 **Find adjectives in the webpage to go with the nouns in the box.**

beauty	music	nature
profession	success	wonder

beauty – *beautiful*

5 **Choose three adjectives from Exercise 4 and write sentences about your life. Compare with a partner.**

I want to be a professional actor when I'm older.

6 **Voice it!** **Answer the questions.**

1 Do you think summer camps make you a more independent person?

2 Do you think it is important to be independent? Why?

LEARN TO LEARN

Understanding different types of English

Different English-speaking countries use different words and expressions. It's important to recognise different types of English. Make a note of them in your notebook and check in a dictionary if you aren't sure.

7 **Is the webpage in American English or British English?**

8 **Look at the highlighted words in the webpage. Match them with the British English words.**

1 centre *center*
2 football
3 favourite
4 holiday
5 flat
6 theatre

9.11 9 **COLLABORATE** **Match the British English words in A with the American English words in B. Listen and check.**

A ~~autumn~~ chips garden rubber rubbish sweets trousers

B candy eraser ~~fall~~ fries garbage pants yard

autumn – *fall*

Mini [culture] project p136

Search camps > | Age | State | Length | Find a camp now

Languages for Life, Georgia

Learn a new language! Choose from Arabic, Chinese and lots more! You'll live and sleep in the language and culture. You won't speak English for a month! In your free time, why not visit the world's largest aquarium or one of Georgia's wonderful museums?

Advanced Soccer Skills, California

Los Angeles has a long history of sport – the Summer Olympics in 1932 and 1984 and in 2028 the Olympics will be here again! In just one week, our professional coaches will use your natural talent to teach you amazing new soccer skills. Sorry no beginners!

Theater School, New Jersey

New Jersey is home to one of the most successful performing arts centers in the USA. Develop your musical talents or choose from circus skills, magic, public speaking or acting! After two weeks here, you'll perform live on the last day.

9 REVIEW

VOCABULARY

1 Match the verbs with the nouns.

1 use	a a map
2 identify	b a shelter
3 build	c fish
4 catch	d plants
5 read	e a compass

2 Write the words for holiday accommodation.

1 This is part of a larger building. You have your own bedroom, kitchen and bathroom.
2 This is a cheap and simple type of shelter. You don't sleep in a bed.
3 You share a room with other people in this place.
4 You travel and sleep in this and you don't need a car.

GRAMMAR

3 Complete the sentences with *will/won't* and a verb from the box.

have speak win

1 I know you … an amazing holiday in Turkey.
2 She … any English in Russia.
3 … your country … the next World Cup?

4 Complete the conversation with the present continuous form of the verbs.

DAN: Hi, Gabi. What [1]… you … (do) on Saturday?
GABI: I [2]… (meet) Louisa in town. Why?
DAN: Matt and Clara [3]… (come) to my house to organise a surprise party for Gino.
GABI: Really? When [4]… you … (have) the party?
DAN: On 15th September. Can you come?
GABI: I think so. I [5]… (not do) anything that weekend.
DAN: Great!

5 Write sentences with the correct form of *going to*.

1 … they … to a summer camp this year? (go)
2 I … early on Saturday! (not get up)
3 Becca … all the food for the party. (cook)
4 We … in a caravan this summer. (not stay)
5 When … you … your grandparents? (visit)
6 Erdem … footbal next Sunday? (not play)

6 Choose the correct verbs in the sentences.

1 *I'm going to visit / I'll visit* my cousins in Paris next weekend.
2 Which subjects *are you choosing / will you choose* next year?
3 Jack can't come to the cinema tomorrow. *He's working / He'll work*.
4 *Will Kate want / Is Kate wanting* to come to the cinema with us tomorrow?
5 The students *will have / are having* their fashion show next Friday night.
6 *You'll have / You're having* a great time at the camp next week.

Vocabulary

Outdoor life

build a shelter	identify plants
catch fish	light a fire
collect wood	pick fruit
cook over a campfire	read a map
find food and water	use a compass

Holidays

apartment	chalet
B&B (bed & breakfast)	cottage
	hotel
camper van	tent
caravan	youth hostel

Grammar

will/won't
be going to
Present continuous for future

9 FINISHED?

1 **Write clues for the words in the crossword.**

[1] C										
O										
[2] M	A	P								
P									[3] F	
A						[4] F	R	U	I	T
S			[5] P			I			S	
[6] S	H	E	L	T	E	R			H	
			A			E				
			N							
	[7] W	A	T	E	R					
			S							

Across 2 *You need to read this to find your way.*

2 **Use the table to find six holiday words.**

1	2	3	4	5	6	7	8	9	10	11	12	13
A	B	C	D	E	F	G	H	I	J	K	L	M
N	O	P	Q	R	S	T	U	V	W	X	Y	Z

1. 8 2 7 5 12 — *H O T E L*
2. 3 8 1 12 5 7
3. 7 5 1 7
4. 1 3 1 5 7 13 5 1 7
5. 3 1 13 3 5 5 9 1 1
6. 3 2 7 7 1 7 5

3 **What will your life be like in the future? Make predictions with *will* and *won't*. Use the ideas below or your own ideas.**

I won't live in an apartment, I'll live in a very big house.

4 **Look at the reminder notes and write two sentences for each person. Use the present continuous and *going to*.**

Tomorrow Javier is going to try to book concert tickets. He's having lunch with Fiona at 12.30.

Tomorrow: Try to book concert tickets. Lunch with Fiona 12.30.
Javier

Saturday afternoon: Drive into town with Mum – buy new jeans
Magda

Monday: Meet Josef at the café – give him his birthday present
Rachel and Sam

Tuesday: Guitar lesson, 5.30–6.30. Call Dad from the station.
Luis

Friday: Visit the science museum: bus leaving school 8:15. Don't be late!!
Leo

UNIT REVIEW 7–9

FUNCTIONAL LANGUAGE

SPEAKING

Everyday English

UNIT 7

No way!
Really?
Wow!
You're joking!

UNIT 8

Calm down.
Don't panic!
Gross!
Let's think.

UNIT 9

Easy!
Forget that.
I don't believe it!
I'm on it!
You're unbelievable!!

Useful Language

UNIT 7

How was (the school trip)?
It was (amazing)!
What about (lions)?
What was (it) like?

UNIT 8

Did you have it when you (got to school)?
Did you put it (in your bag)?
What did you do with it after that?
When did you last (have/use/see) it?

UNIT 9

Making suggestions

What about a (film night)?
What are we going to do?
Why don't we (have a picnic)?
I'm not sure about that.
I'd rather not do that.
Let's do that!

WRITING

Useful Language

UNIT 7

Writing a biography

On 10 October 2005
When she was two months old
In 2007
A few years ago
Today

UNIT 8

Writing a blog post

I didn't hear my alarm **so** I got up late.

UNIT 9

Writing an email

in the morning, in June, on Monday, on 1st August at home, at the airport

VOCABULARY

1 **Correct the sentences.**

1 Parrots are very quiet birds.
2 Crocodiles are cute slow and dangerous.
3 Giraffes are carnivores and lions are herbivores.
4 You can buy a bus pass at the market.
5 Isaac is going to send a letter at the library.
6 I've got a passport for the theatre tonight.
7 Doctors at the hospital wear ID keys.
8 We need to open a fire so we don't get cold.
9 They are taking fruit in the garden.
10 We're staying at the youth hotel this weekend.

GRAMMAR

2 Read the dialogue and choose the correct option.

LAURA: Hi Daniel! Did you enjoy your trip to the wildlife park?
DANIEL: Yes, I [1]… , thanks. I saw lots of bears and snakes.
LAURA: [2]… there any lions? I love lions!
DANIEL: No, there [3]… . But there were some tigers.
LAURA: Wow! Did you [4]… them close?
DANIEL: No, I [5]… . They were really far away!
LAURA: Oh no, really! [6]… did you go with?
DANIEL: I [7]… with my mum and dad.
LAURA: [8]… you tell us about it in English class today?
DANIEL: Yes, [9]… going to give a presentation with some photos.
LAURA: Great! We're [10]… presentations in our Science class next week.
DANIEL: And what is yours [11]… be about?
LAURA: I don't know! But I think yours is [12]… to be more interesting!

1	a do	b did	c was
2	a Were	b Was	c Are
3	a wasn't	b weren't	c didn't
4	a see	b saw	c look
5	a wasn't	b don't	c didn't
6	a Who	b When	c What
7	a went	b go	c been
8	a Are	b Will	c Do
9	a I will	b I	c I'm
10	a give	b giving	c gave
11	a going to	b are	c will
12	a is	b will	c going

Take the challenge!

1 Answer the questions. What can you do at the …
1 ice rink?
2 aquarium?
3 stadium?
4 sports centre?

2 Match the words in box A with words in box B.

A	B
build	a map
catch	fish
identify	a compass
read	plants
use	a shelter

3 Complete the questions with your ideas. Then ask a partner and write down their answers.
1 Where did you / last weekend?
2 Who did you / with this morning?
3 What did you / yesterday?

4 Think about your last summer holiday. Complete the sentences about the place.
1 There was … .
2 There wasn't … .
3 There were … .
4 There weren't any … .

5 Write four sentences about next week. Use the present continuous or *be going to*.

6 COLLABORATE Swap your sentences with a partner. Are you going to do anything similar?

1 MINI CULTURE PROJECT

A poster

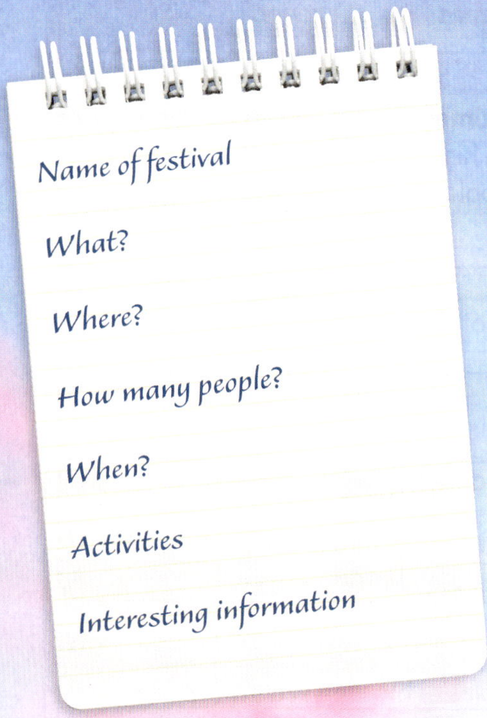

How to design a poster

Remember to think about the following ideas.

- Organise your information and remember to select the most important or interesting ideas.
- Include a short, but interesting title for your poster.
- Give your poster a border to make it more attractive.
- Select one big attractive photo or drawing as the main focus, but also include small photos, maps and drawings.
- Make sure your handwriting is clear and use some bright colours, if possible.
- Check your grammar, punctuation and spelling before you finish.

TASK

Design a poster

PLAN

1 **Work in groups. Choose a festival from around the world and find information about it. Then complete the steps below.**

- Write the name of the festival.
- Look at the notebook and complete the information for your festival. Then make a spidergram.

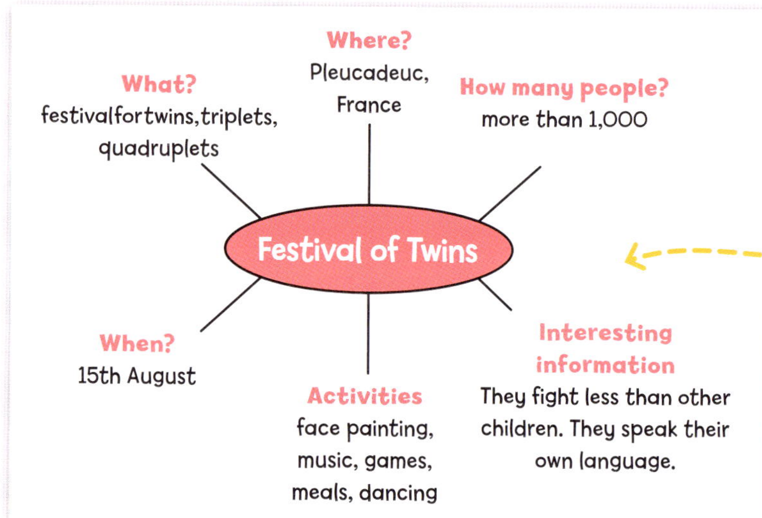

- Decide on who prepares each section.
- Decide on the design of your poster.
- Prepare your section. Use photos, maps, drawings, etc.
- Give your section to someone in your group to check.
- Work in your group to put the whole poster together.

PRESENT

2 **Present your poster to the class. Don't forget to include the items in the** CHECKLIST**.**

CHECKLIST **Remember to include:**

- facts about the festival
- photos, maps and drawings etc.
- the tips from *How to* design a poster.

CHECK

3 COLLABORATE **Look at your classmates' posters. Do they use the items in the** CHECKLIST**? Which is your favourite poster? Why?**

FESTIVAL OF TWINS

Come to the Festival of Twins! All twins, triplets and quadruplets are welcome!
Come and have a fun day out, with your family and friends and meet new friends!

Where and when?

In the beautiful town of Pleucadeuc on 15th August.

Join in with our fun activities:

dancing face painting games meals music

• More than 1,000 people come every year!

TWIN FACTS

Did you know?

Twins fight less than other children. Twins speak their own language.

3 MINI CULTURE PROJECT

A haiku

A haiku is a short Japanese poem with three lines. The first line has got five syllables, the second line has got seven and the last line has got five. That's a total of 17 syllables. The lines don't rhyme.

1 2 3 4 5

1 2 3 4 5 6 7

1 2 3 4 5

How to speak to a large group

Remember to think about the following ideas.

- Introduce yourself.
- Wait for everyone to be quiet so you can start speaking.
- Take a deep breath before you speak!
- Try to stand still when speaking.
- Look at your audience.
- Remember to smile!
- Speak slowly and clearly, and make sure everyone can hear you.
- Enjoy what you are saying.
- Time your presentation.

TASK

Write a haiku

PLAN

1 Work with a group or on your own. Choose a topic you like from the box or choose your own topic. Then complete the steps below.

animals	friends	love	music	nature
school	the five senses	the weather		

- Think about your topic – how does it make you feel?
- Draw some pictures or find some photos about your topic to inspire you.
- Brainstorm as many words as you can about the topic and include some of your feelings.
- Choose your favourite words.
- Organise your words into sentences. Remember to count the syllables in each line.
- Check the number of syllables in each line and change words, if necessary.
- Write the final version of your haiku.

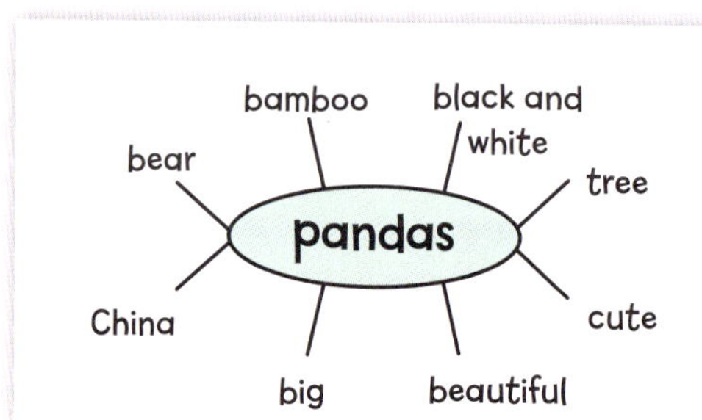

PRESENT

2 When you are happy with your haiku, read it to the class. Don't forget to include the items in the CHECKLIST**.**

CHECKLIST **Remember to include:**

- words related to your topic
- three lines with the correct number of syllables
- the tips from *How to* speak to a large group.

CHECK

3 COLLABORATE **Listen to your classmates' haikus. Do they use the items in the** CHECKLIST**? Which is your favourite haiku? Who or what is it about?**

Black and white panda
Come down from your tree and see
The bamboo for you.

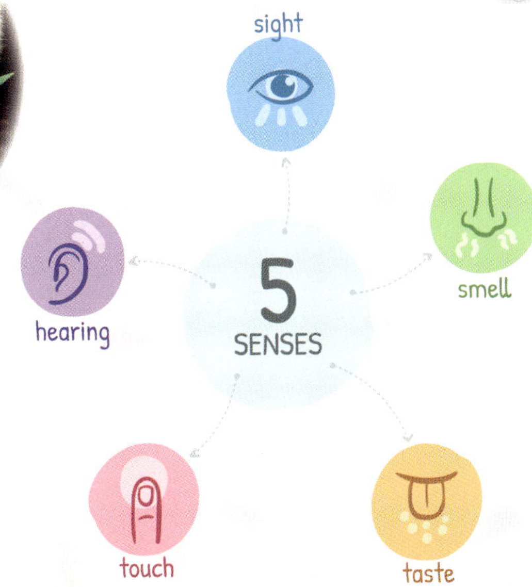

We have five of them
To see, hear, taste, touch and smell
They help us to live.

The leaves on the trees
Are falling to the ground now
It's autumn again.

We study at school
History, music and English
Art, drama and more.

My friends are the best
They make me laugh and feel good
Have you got a friend?

5 MINI CULTURE PROJECT

A lookbook

How to present a project

Remember to think about the following ideas.

- Introduce yourselves to the class.
- Make sure you know who is going to say what in your group.
- Make sure you have everything you need to present your project.
- Try to remember what you are going to say and don't read from your notes!
- Don't interrupt other people in your group – wait for them to finish talking.
- Always look at your audience when you are speaking.
- Remember to speak slowly and clearly!
- At the end, ask if there are any questions and be prepared to answer them.
- Time your presentation.

TASK

Make a lookbook

PLAN

1 **Work in groups. Choose a style of clothes that you like. Then complete the steps below.**

- Find out as much information as you can about the style.
- Make a spidergram with the style of clothes and the vocabulary you need.

clothes
long skirt and top (lehenga), sari, scarf (dupatta)

Hindu bride's outfit

accessories
earrings, flowers for hair, bracelets, nose ring, shoes, hair pins, ankle chain, toe ring, necklace

- Take or find photos or draw pictures of the people wearing the clothes and accessories.
- Decide on who prepares each section.
- Decide on the design of your lookbook.
- Prepare your section. Write sentences about each of the pictures and what the people are wearing.
- Give your section to someone in your group to check.
- Work in your group to put the lookbook together.

PRESENT

2 **Present your lookbook to the class. Don't forget to include the items in the CHECKLIST.**

CHECKLIST **Remember to include:**

- photos or drawings
- sentences about what the people are wearing
- the tips from *How to* present a project.

CHECK

3 COLLABORATE **Listen to your classmates' presentations. Do they use the items in the CHECKLIST? Which is your favourite lookbook? Why? Have a class vote and decide on the best lookbook.**

earrings

flowers

nose ring

bracelets

lehenga

scarf

necklace

shoes

The model is wearing a beautiful gold and red long skirt and top, a lehenga, with a traditional scarf or dupatta, with gold and red flowers on it. She is wearing lots of different accessories including gold earrings and a diamond necklace. She is also wearing lots of gold bracelets on both arms and rings on her fingers. She looks amazing!

7 MINI CULTURE PROJECT

A scrapbook

How to design a scrapbook

Remember to think about the following ideas.

- Make sure you use some bright colours.
- Remember to include photos and drawings.
- Decide on the format in your group.
- Choose a clear font (if you're doing it on a computer) or write neatly.
- Make sure you write full sentences to describe the photos and drawings in your scrapbook.

TASK

Make a scrapbook

PLAN

1 **Work in groups. Imagine you visited a friend in another part of the world last week. Choose the place that you visited, then complete the steps below.**

- Decide on the design of your scrapbook: digital or paper?
- Find photos of people, animals, buildings and monuments in the place you visited.

- Find out as much information as you can about your photos.
- Decide on who prepares each section.
- Prepare your section. Write sentences about each of the pictures, what the people are doing and what you saw.
- Give your section to someone in your group to check.
- Work in your group to put the scrapbook together.

PRESENT

2 **Present your scrapbook to another group. Don't forget to include the items in the CHECKLIST.**

CHECKLIST **Remember to include:**

- different photos of people, animals and places
- sentences to describe your photos
- the tips from *How to* design a scrapbook.

CHECK

3 COLLABORATE **Look at your classmates' scrapbooks. Do they use the items in the CHECKLIST? Whose trip was the most exciting? Why?**

Our trip to the Altai Mountains

The Altai Mountains are beautiful and very big. We stayed there for a week and had lots of fun! There was a lot of snow!

This is Ganzorig. He's four. We met him at the Golden Eagle Festival in the Altai Mountains. He played with the bird in the photo all day!

This is Enkhtuya's golden eagle. Enkhutya is Ganzorig's sister and Batbayar's daughter. She is an eagle huntress and she entered the competition last year. She wanted to win, but she didn't!

We ate with Batbayar's family every evening. The food was delicious. We didn't sit on chairs – we sat on the floor. There were about 30 people in Batbayar's house to eat. The people were very friendly.

The Altai Mountains were beautiful. There were lots of animals, like eagles and horses at the Golden eagle competition. Everyone had a good time.

There were also reindeer! They were very friendly!

9 MINI CULTURE PROJECT

A webpage

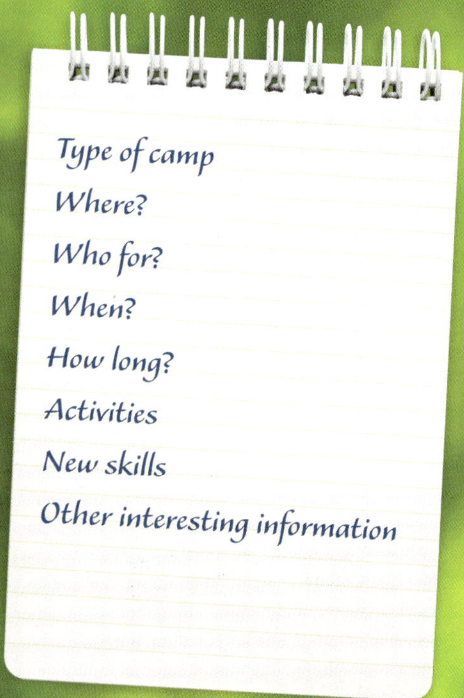

How to make a webpage

Remember to think about the following ideas.

- Choose an interesting and relevant name for your webpage. Remember you want lots of people to visit it.
- Make sure your webpage is attractive, use photos and descriptions
- Make sure your webpage is easy to use.
- Organise the information you want to include carefully.
- Include photos, maps and drawings.
- Include contact details.

TASK

Make a summer camp webpage

PLAN

1 **Work in groups. Decide what your summer camp is and give it a name or use one of the ideas in the box. Then complete the steps below.**

cooking	sport	drama	music	adventure

- Look at the notebook and complete the information for your summer camp. Then make a spidergram.

- Find an online template for your webpage.
- Organise your information and decide on who will prepare each section.
- Prepare your section. Use photos, maps, drawings, etc.
- Give your section to someone in your group to check.
- Work in your group to put the webpage together.

PRESENT

2 **Present your webpage to the class. Answer any questions your classmates have. Don't forget to include the items in the CHECKLIST.**

CHECKLIST **Remember to include:**

- information about the camp
- photos, maps and drawings, etc.
- the tips from *How to* design a webpage.

CHECK

3 COLLABORATE **Look at your classmates' webpages. Do they use the items in the CHECKLIST? Which camp do you think is the most interesting? Which is the best webpage? Why?**

Crazy Cook Camp

What is it?

A cookery camp, where you will learn how to cook delicious meals, make new friends from around the world, learn a little Spanish and above all, have fun!

Where is the camp?

Madrid

Who is it for?

Children from 10–16 years old

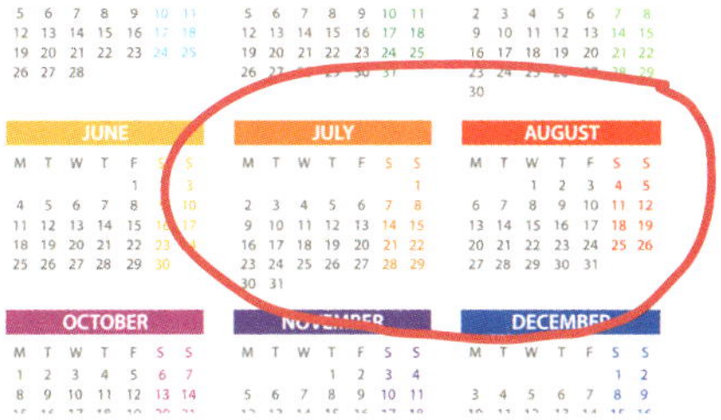

When is the camp?

In the months of July and August

How long is the camp?

You can stay for one week, two weeks, three weeks or even a month!

What will I do on the camp?

You will cook, have free time to relax, visit places in the amazing city of Madrid, eat in top restaurants around the capital of Spain, meet famous chefs, have a day out at the fun fair, take part in different competitions, win prizes, play different sports and much, much more!

What will I learn?

You'll learn to cook, you'll make new friends for life, you'll learn about food from around the world and you'll become the best chef in your family!

Contact us: for more information, click here

2 MATHS

1 When do you use maths in your daily activities?

2 Read and listen to the article. Are any of your ideas from Exercise 1 in the article? 2.14

3 Match the words in **bold** in the text with the examples.

1 1 kg, two cups …
2 7/8, 4/5 …
3 45%, 99% …

4 Read the article again and look at the pictures. Answer the questions in blue.

5 Are the sentences *T* (true) or *F* (false)?

1 We don't need fractions in real life. F
2 We use maths every time we tell the time.
3 'A quarter' and 'half' are examples of percentages.

Explore it!

Do the calculation.

Write the number of the month you were born. Multiply by 4. Add 13. Multiply by 25. Subtract 200. Add the day of the month you were born. Multiply by 2. Subtract 40. Multiply by 50. Add the last two numbers of the year you were born. Subtract 10,500.

The first two numbers are the month you were born. The next two numbers are the day you were born. The last two numbers are the year you were born.

Find an interesting maths puzzle and test your partner.

Everyday Maths

Your maths teacher gives you homework on fractions. 'I don't need **fractions** in real life,' you think. 'What's the point?' In fact, maths is everywhere.

Telling the Time

'Excuse me, what time is it?' someone asks. You look at your phone. 'It's a quarter to four,' you reply. This is a really mathematical sentence, and you need to know about fractions! **How many minutes are there in the fractions 'a quarter', 'half' and 'three-quarters'?**

Shopping

You want some new clothes, so you go shopping. You see something nice and a sign says there is 40% off the original price of £20. Then you see another offer … 50% off the original price of £26. **Which item do you buy?** It helps to know how **percentages** work before you waste money!

Cooking

You want to make your favourite biscuits. The recipe asks for two tablespoons of sugar, but you only have a teaspoon. **How many teaspoons make two tablespoons?** You may know the answer, but that's because you understand maths and **measurements**!

We use maths every day of our lives. So, the next time your maths teacher gives you homework, make sure you do it!

4 ART

1 Look carefully at the photo. What can you see?

2 (4.13) Read and listen to the article and match the foods with what they represent in the photo.

1 broccoli 2 carrot and cheese 3 fruit

3 Are the sentences *T* (true) or *F* (false)?

1 We need to look at the photo again to understand it.
2 The photo shows a dream.
3 Warner makes the photos with other people.
4 He doesn't eat all the food at the end of the session.

4 Check the meaning of the words in **bold** in the article.

Explore it!

Guess the correct answer.

Carl Warner also makes food photos of famous buildings. What is the main ingredient in his photo of the Taj Mahal?

a chicken b onions c bread

Find an interesting fact about food and art. Then write a question for your partner to answer.

Foodscapes

There are many works of art about food. But there are also times when art is food. Literally.

Look at the photo. What can you see? There are some houses and trees. There is a tower, and there are a lot of balloons in the sky. It is a beautiful **landscape**!

Now look again. That isn't a tower … it is a carrot on some cheese! Those aren't trees … they are pieces of broccoli! And those balloons are all different types of fruit!

Don't worry, you are not dreaming. Photographer Carl Warner loves making landscapes out of food because he loves their connection with the natural world. He calls them 'foodscapes' and the results are amazing.

Warner takes three days to prepare a photograph. First, he decides which ingredients to use. Then he builds the **scene** with his team. Next, he takes photos in **layers**. There is a lot of **fresh** food, so he works quickly under the hot lights. What happens to the food at the end of a session? He shares it with his team, of course!

First, Warner wants to make people smile. However, he also wants to promote a good diet. With these **surreal** images, he makes us think about food in a different way.

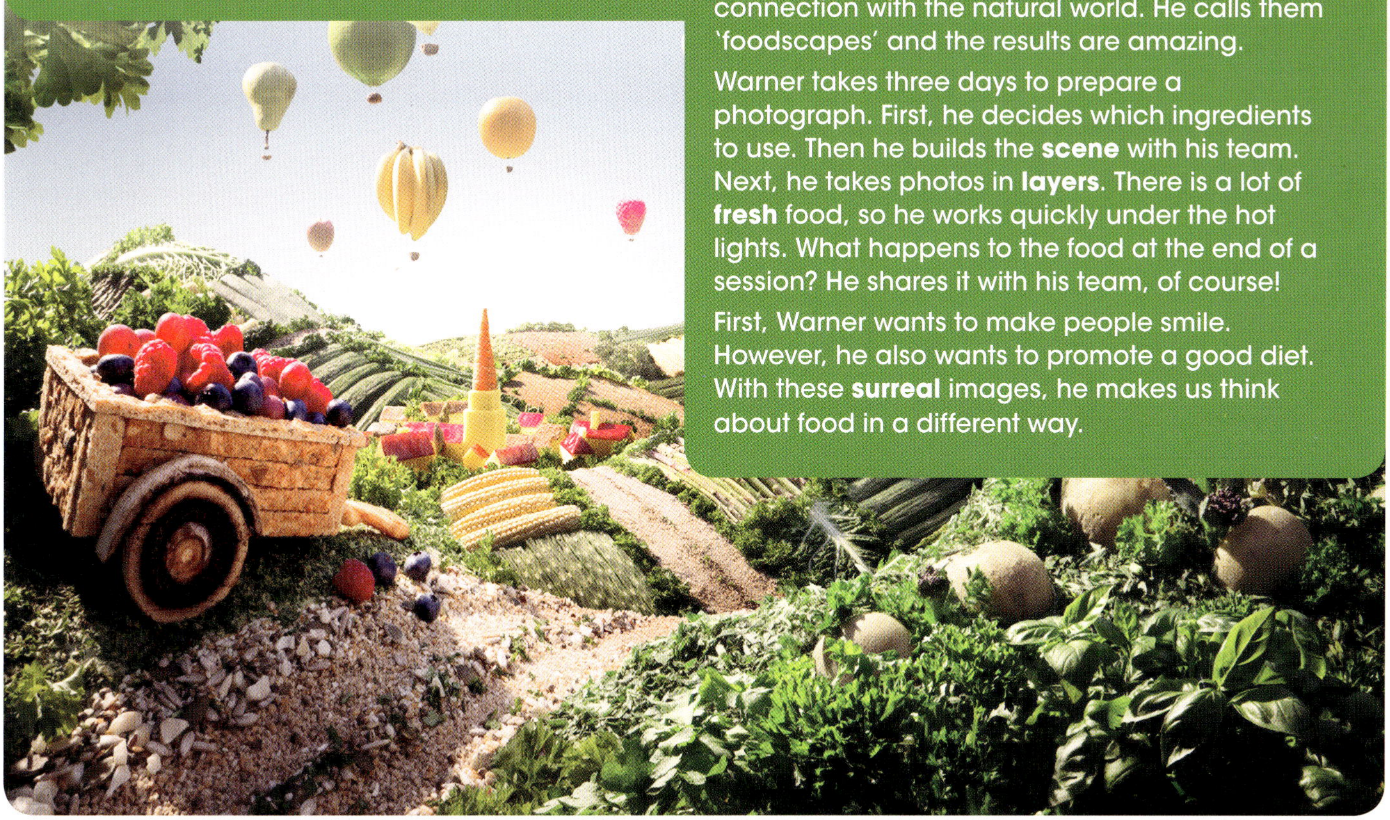

6 PE

1 Discuss the questions.

1 Which sports do you do?

2 Which of these skills do you need to have in your favourite sport?

bouncing catching jumping kicking teamwork

6.12 2 **Read and listen to the article. Check the meaning of the words in bold. Then match them with the definitions.**

1 … : *v* to practise a sport

2 … : *n* the ability to do something difficult for a long time

3 … : *adj* very strong

3 **Read the article again and match the sentence halves.**

1 Olga and Maya are

2 Type I muscle tissue is

3 Type II muscle tissue gets

4 Maya has got

a more Type II muscle tissue that Olga.

b both runners.

c better for stamina.

d tired fast.

4 **Make a list of activities that use slow-twitch and fast-twitch muscles. Use the ones in the box and add your own ideas.**

American football bicycle racing bossaball rock climbing surfing

slow-twitch fast-twitch

Explore it!

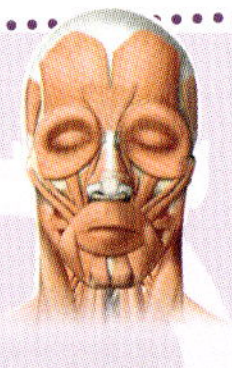

Guess the correct answer.

What's the fastest muscle in the body?

a eye b tongue c finger

Find an interesting fact about muscles. Then write a question for your partner to answer.

FAST OR SLOW?

Meet Olympic sportspeople Olga and Maya. They have a lot in common, but they are also very different.

Olga competes in an event with three different parts: the triathlon. She swims 1.5 km, then cycles 40 km and finishes with a 10-km run!

Maya runs the 100-metre race. She is much faster than Olga. But she cannot do a triathlon.

Olga has got more **stamina** and Maya has got more speed. But why? What's different inside their bodies?

The difference is in the types of muscles they use.

Type I muscle tissue (slow-twitch)

This muscle doesn't have a lot of power, but it can keep going. Marathon runners use Type I muscle tissue.

Type II muscle tissue (fast-twitch)

This is much more **powerful**, but it gets tired fast – in less than a minute. Sprinters use Type II muscle tissue.

Now, the difference is obvious. Olga **trains** her slow-twitch muscles more and Maya has a lot more fast-twitch muscle.

SO, WHICH IS BETTER?

WHICH MUSCLES HAVE YOU GOT MORE OF?

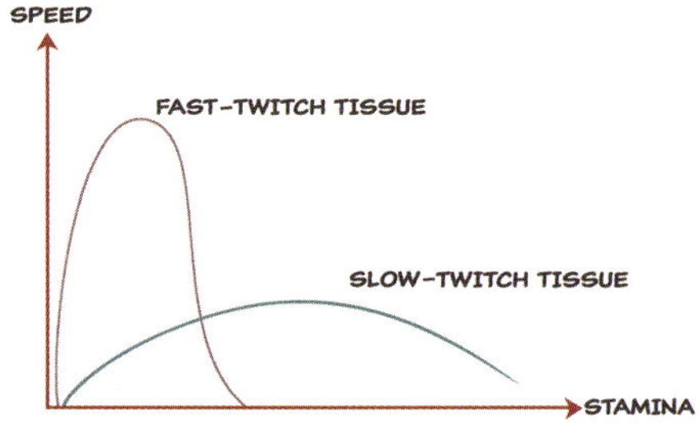

8 HISTORY

1 How old are the paintings in the picture?

2 Read and listen to the article. Check your ideas to Exercise 1.

8.13

3 Find the synonyms in **bold** in the text.

1 amazing
2 hole
3 profound
4 something you find

4 Match the questions (a–f) with the paragraphs (1–6) in the text.

a What did they find?
b Did the boys keep their promise?
c Where did the boys make the discovery?
d How did the boys feel?
e When did the discovery take place?
f How did they make the discovery?

5 Read the article again and put the events in order.

a The boys saw a hole in the ground.
b Archaeologists came to see the paintings.
c The boys saw pictures of animals in a cave.
d The boys threw stones down a hole.

Explore it!

Guess the correct answer.

Cave artists used … as paint.

a blood b charcoal c food

Find an interesting fact about the Lascaux cave paintings. Then write a question for your partner to answer.

The Lascaux Cave Paintings

1 …

On 12 September 1940 four teenage boys made an amazing discovery. What do you think they discovered? Read on to find out …

2 …

The boys were in the woods near the village of Montignac, France. One of them, Marcel Ravidat, saw a hole in the ground a few days earlier. They believed it was the entrance to a secret tunnel that people in the village talked about.

3 …

First, they looked inside the hole. Then they threw stones through the **opening** to see how **deep** it was. They decided to go in and carefully climbed down fifteen metres. At the bottom there was a cave. They were amazed by what they saw.

4 …

There were **incredible** paintings all over the walls, including hundreds of pictures of red, black, brown and yellow animals. The animals looked like they were moving in the dark.

5 …

The boys were excited but also worried about getting out. They left the cave and promised to keep their **discovery** a secret.

6 …

No, the whole village soon found out, and archaeologists came to visit. The cave paintings were about 17,000 years old. Can you imagine that? They are still some of the best examples of prehistoric art ever discovered.

PRONUNCIATION

UNIT 1

/h/

1.07 **1 Listen and repeat.**

/h/ have got Hey! home husband

1.08 **2 Listen and choose the option you hear.**

1 hat / at
2 hair / air
3 has / as
4 hand / and

1.09 **3 Listen and repeat the sentences.**

1 Hunter has got brown hair and he is happy.
2 Hey! How are things?

4 Practise saying the sentences in Exercise 3.

UNIT 2

/s/, /z/ and /ɪz/

2.05 **1 Listen and repeat.**

/s/ speak**s** /z/ doe**s** /ɪz/ chang**es**

2.06 **2 Listen and write A (/s/ or /z/) or B (/ɪz/).**

1 goes
2 studies
3 eats
4 teaches

3 Add *-s* or *-es* to the verbs and put them in the correct column.

break catch choose go read think watch

/s/ or /z/	/ɪz/

2.07 **4 Listen, check and repeat.**

5 Cover the table in Exercise 3 and take turns to say a verb from the box. You partner says the verb with the *-s* ending.

UNIT 3

can

3.03 **1 Listen and repeat.**

1 /kən/ She can play the piano.
2 /kən/ Can he read music?
3 /kæn/ Yes, he can.
4 /kɑːnt/ She can't go.

3.04 **2 Listen and choose the option you hear.**

1 I *can* / *can't* hear you.
2 Pablo *can* / *can't* help you with your homework.
3 They *can* / *can't* count to 20 in Russian.
4 *Can* / *Can't* you use your phone at school?

3 Read the conversation. Write the numbers (1–7) in the correct column.

/kən/	/kæn/	/kɑːnt/

BETH: Hi, Tim. [1]Can I ask you some questions?
TIM: Yes, you [2]can. Of course.
BETH: Great. [3]Can you swim?
TIM: No, I [4]can't.
BETH: [5]Can you draw or paint?
TIM: Yes, I [6]can.
BETH: And [7]can you speak Spanish?
TIM: *Sí*! I mean yes.

3.05 **4 Listen and check.**

5 Practise the conversation in Exercise 3.

UNIT 4

Word stress

1 How many syllables have these words got?

apples disgusting salty unhealthy vegetable water

4.06 **2 Listen and check.**

3 Match the words in Exercise 1 with the stress patterns (1–3).

1 Oo
2 oOo
3 Ooo

4.07 **4 Listen, check and repeat.**

5 Mark the stress on these words. Choose the odd one out in each group.

1 sugar / carrots / bananas / chicken
2 delicious / disgusting / unhealthy / difficult

4.08 6 Listen and check.

UNIT 5

-ing

5.03 1 Listen and repeat.

play**ing** stand**ing** sing**ing**

5.04 2 Match the sentence halves. Then listen, check and repeat.

1 Martin is writing a around the world.
2 Amir is catching b salsa.
3 Ysabella is travelling c a letter.
4 Oscar is dancing d fish in the sea.

3 Practise saying the sentences in Exercise 2.

UNIT 6

Schwa /ə/

6.04 1 Listen and repeat.

better bigger easier faster happier
healthier older smaller smarter

2 Match the words in Exercise 1 with the stress patterns. Write 1 or 2.

1 Oo 2 Ooo

6.05 3 Listen and repeat the sentences. How many schwa /ə/ sounds do you hear?

1 Jane is smaller than her sister.
2 Bossaball is better than football.
3 My brother is happier now he plays rugby.

4 Practise saying the sentences in Exercise 3.

UNIT 7

/t/, /d/ and /ɪd/

7.07 1 Listen and repeat.

/t/ lik**ed** /d/ play**ed** /ɪd/ want**ed**

7.08 2 Listen and write A (/t/ or /d/) or B (/ɪd/).

1 looked 2 wanted 3 danced 4 needed

3 Write the past simple form of the verbs in the box and put them in the correct place in the table.

call climb hunt start want watch

/t/ **or** /d/	/ɪd/

7.09 4 Listen, check and repeat.

5 Cover the table in Exercise 3 and take turns to say a verb from the box. Your partner says the past form of the verb. Check your partner's pronunciation.

UNIT 8

Intonation in questions

8.03 1 Listen and repeat.

1 Did Pablo move house?
2 Did they go to the swimming pool yesterday?
3 Did you visit your grandma in hospital?

2 Mark where your voice goes up in the questions.

1 Did Alex play basketball at the sports centre?
2 Did you take the letter to the post office?
3 Did Fred and George buy anything?
4 Did your brother go to the library?
5 Did Evie and Jake go to the skate park on Friday?

8.04 3 Listen, check and repeat.

UNIT 9

going to

9.07 1 Listen and repeat.

1 What are you **going to** do?
2 I'm **going to** watch a film.

9.08 2 Listen and choose the option you hear.

1 He's *going to* / *gonna* order pizza.
2 Are they *going to* / *gonna* travel to Turkey?
3 I'm not *going to* / *gonna* tell you the secret.
4 Are you *going to* / *gonna* help me?
5 She's *going to* / *gonna* buy a new T-shirt.
6 Is he *going to* / *gonna* talk to the teacher?

3 Practise saying the sentences in Exercise 2.

IRREGULAR VERBS

Infinitive	Past simple	Past participle
be	was / were	been
beat	beat	beaten
become	became	become
begin	began	begun
break	broke	broken
bring	brought	brought
build	built	built
buy	bought	bought
catch	caught	caught
choose	chose	chosen
come	came	come
cost	cost	cost
cut	cut	cut
do	did	done
draw	drew	drawn
drink	drank	drunk
drive	drove	driven
eat	ate	eaten
fall	fell	fallen
feel	felt	felt
fight	fought	fought
find	found	found
fly	flew	flown
forget	forgot	forgotten
get	got	got
give	gave	given
go	went	gone
grow	grew	grown
have	had	had
hear	heard	heard
hide	hid	hidden
hit	hit	hit
hold	held	held
keep	kept	kept

Infinitive	Past simple	Past participle
know	knew	known
leave	left	left
lose	lost	lost
make	made	made
meet	met	met
pay	paid	paid
put	put	put
read	read	read
ride	rode	ridden
ring	rang	rung
run	ran	run
say	said	said
see	saw	seen
sell	sold	sold
send	sent	sent
show	showed	shown
shut	shut	shut
sing	sang	sung
sit	sat	sat
sleep	slept	slept
speak	spoke	spoken
spend	spent	spent
stand	stood	stood
swim	swam	swum
take	took	taken
teach	taught	taught
tell	told	told
think	thought	thought
throw	threw	thrown
understand	understood	understood
wake	woke	woken
wear	wore	worn
win	won	won
write	wrote	written

KEY COMPETENCIES PRACTICE

LEARN TO ... ORGANISE YOUR NOTEBOOK

It's important to organise your notebook to help you to find your notes and study for exams.

1 Ask and answer with a partner.

1. Have you got a notebook?
2. Is it for all your subjects or for English only?
3. Are your notes easy or difficult to read?

2 Match the words in the box with a–d in Omar's notebook.

vocabulary ~~date~~ homework grammar

a date

a 23 September

b

have got	
I / you / we / they	have / haven't got ...
he / she / it	has / hasn't got ...

c

Family members	
dad	mum
husband	wife
brother	sister
son	daughter
uncle	aunt
nephew	niece
grandad	grandma
grandson	granddaughter
cousin	cousin

d Learn the family words from Unit 1.

Search online for a digital sticky note board. Try and use it to organise your notebook. Share your findings with your classmates.

3 Look at Azra's notebook. Is her notebook different from Omar's? How?

grammar

vocabulary

notes

homework

Verb *be*

Affirmative	Negative	Questions
I'm from Turkey.	I'm not from Turkey.	Am I Brazilian?
She's my sister.	She isn't my sister.	Is she Mexican?
He's my brother.	He isn't my brother.	Is he from Ecuador?
We're at school.	We aren't at school.	Are we 12?
They're my cousins.	They aren't my cousins.	Are they at school?

4 Ask and answer with a partner.

1. What is good about Omar's notebook? What is good about Azra's?
2. What are some other ways to organise a notebook?
3. Which is your favourite way? Why?

5 Discuss with a partner. Decide how to organise your notebook.

LEARN TO ... WORK IN PAIRS

When you work in pairs, you learn from your partner.

1 In your notebook, complete the advice 1–6 with *Always* or *Never*.

Let's work well together!

1 ... listen to your partner.

2 ... answer your partner's questions.

3 ... speak at the same time as your partner.

4 ... help your partner with words they don't know.

5 ... laugh at your partner's mistakes.

6 ... ask questions to get more information.

1 Always

2 Ask and answer questions with a partner. In your notebook, complete sentences 1–4. Practise the advice in Exercise 1.

1 We both like ….
2 My partner likes … but I don't.
3 I like … but my partner doesn't.
4 We don't like ….

Do you like hanging out with friends?

Yes, I do.

Me, too. Let's write 'hanging out with friends' in sentence 1.

3 In your notebook, complete the sentences about how you work in pairs with *always*, *sometimes* or *never*.

When I work in pairs …

1 I always listen to my partner.
2 I … answer my partner's questions.
3 I … speak at the same time as my partner.
4 I … help my partner with words they don't know.
5 I … laugh at my partner's mistakes.
6 I … ask questions to get more information.

4 Tell your partner your sentences from Exercise 3. Do they agree? Why / Why not?

I always listen to my partner.

Hmm. You sometimes listen to your partner.

Search online for a digital mind mapping tool. Try and use it to write down and organise your ideas. Share them with your classmates and learn from their feedback.

LEARN TO LEARN

LEARN TO ... USE FLASHCARDS

Flashcards can help you remember new vocabulary.

1 Match the front and back of the flashcards.

1 information and ______ technology (ICT)

2 

3 hang ______ with friends

4 a place where you do experiments

5 

1 d

a science lab

b glasses

c moustache

d communication

e out

physical ______

2 Which types of flashcard can you see in Exercise 1?

1 picture + word
2 phrase with one word missing
3 word in English + word in your language
4 word + meaning
5 word + example sentence

3 Choose five words or phrases from Unit 3. Use the words or phrases to make the five different types of flashcards in Exercise 2.

4 Show the front of your flashcards from Exercise 3 to your partner. Can they guess what is on the back of each flashcard?

Physical ... Oh, I don't know!

It's a school subject.

Physical education!

Yes! That's right!

5 Discuss with your partner. Which is your favourite type of flashcard from Exercise 2? Why?

Create a digital dictionary. Add chosen words and phrases to it as you finish each unit. Share your findings with your classmates.

LEARN TO LEARN

LEARN TO ... PLAY VOCABULARY GAMES

Games can help you practise and remember new language.

1 Ask and answer with a partner.

1 What games do you like to play?
2 What is your favourite game?
3 Do you play any games to practise English?

2 Work in pairs. Play Word Wizard.

1 Your partner chooses a letter of the alphabet. *a*

2 Write all the food or drink words you know beginning with the letter in 1 minute. Don't show your partner. *apples...*

3 Compare your lists. You get 5 points for a word on both lists. You get 10 points for a word on only your list.

4 Play the game again. This time you choose the letter of the alphabet.

5 The person with the most points is the **Word Wizard**.

3 Work in pairs. Play Three Clues.

Player A: Think of a food or drink. Don't say it! Give Player B three clues.

Player B: After each clue, guess Player A's word. Start with 3 points. Lose 1 point for each wrong guess.

Take turns to be **Player A** and **Player B**. The player with the most points at the end of the game is the winner.

Clue 1. They're healthy. — *Vegetables.*

No! Clue 2. They're sweet. — *Bananas!*

No. Last clue. Sometimes they're green and sometimes they're red. — *Apples!*

Yes, apples! You get 1 point!

4 Three Clues or Word Wizard?

1 Which game practises food nouns?
2 Which game practises food adjectives and food nouns?

5 Discuss with a partner. Think of word games you play in your language. Can you play them in English?

Search online for vocabulary games. Try and play different vocabulary games from the ones you know. Share your findings with your classmates.

LEARN TO LEARN

LEARN TO ... GUESS THE MEANING OF WORDS

When you don't know a word, you can guess the meaning. This helps you to read and listen in English.

1 Which answers are true for you? Compare and discuss your answers with a partner.

When I see a word I don't know, I usually ...

1 guess the meaning.
2 ask the teacher what it means.
3 look in a dictionary.
4 write it in my notebook.

2 Read the text. Discuss the questions about each of the words in **bold** with a partner.

I don't like tight jeans. I prefer **baggy** jeans because they're comfortable. I have lots of T-shirts, T-shirts with long **sleeves**, T-shirts with short **sleeves**, but I don't like T-shirts with **logos** – I don't like pictures or writing on my clothes. I love trainers. I have big feet so it can be difficult to find my size, but my new trainers **fit** really well. They're the perfect size!

YUSUF

1 Are they nouns, verbs or adjectives?

I think 'baggy' is an adjective.

2 What clues about the meaning can you find in the text?

Baggy jeans are not tight.
Baggy jeans are comfortable.

3 What do you think each of the words in **bold** means?

I think 'baggy' means not tight.

3 Read the text. Answer the questions in Exercise 2 about each of the words in **bold**.

I never wear rings, bracelets or earrings, because I don't like **jewellery**, but I have lots of hats, gloves and scarves. Why? Well, my grandma loves to make me clothes – she especially loves to **knit** me clothes. I'm happy about this, because I like to be **warm** on cold winter days, and woollen clothes are great for that!

NIKITA

Search online for different strategies for learning vocabulary. Use at least three of them and share your findings with your classmates.

LEARN TO ... WRITE EXAMPLE SENTENCES

Example sentences help you understand and remember vocabulary

1 Read Peiyu's blog. How does she remember new words? Why?

https:\\peiyusenglishlearningblog.co.uk

Today's tip

Peiyu's English learning blog

Remembering new words

When I learn new words, I use them in example sentences. I think this is better than writing them in my language. When I write sentences, I think about what the word means and this helps me to remember it.

Also, when you write example sentences, the meaning is easier to remember later because the other words in the sentence can help you. I try to write funny sentences or sentences about me and my friends because it's easier to remember the sentences.

Look at my notebook! What do you think?

My parents **do yoga** in the garden.

I **run** to school when I'm late.

2 Choose the example sentences you prefer, a or b. Compare your answers with a partner and say why.

1 bananas
- a Bananas are nice.
- (b) Bananas are a long yellow fruit.

I prefer example sentence b because the words 'long', 'yellow' and 'fruit' help you remember what bananas are.

2 kick
- a In football, players kick a ball.
- b They kick it.

3 rugby
- a Rugby is my grandma's favourite sport.
- b Rugby is boring.

4 throw
- a Throw it!
- b My baby sister throws her food at me.

3 Write an example sentence for each of the words in the box.

beat catch rock climbing score volleyball

4 Tell your partner your sentences from Exercise 3. Who has the best example sentence for each word?

I prefer your sentence for 'beat' because it's funny.

Search online for other examples of tips people use to remember things. Try and use a different website from the one you normally use. Share your findings with your classmates.

LEARN TO ... USE MIND MAPS

Mind maps can help you think of ideas and plan how to organise them.

1 Discuss the questions.

1 What is a mind map?
2 Why do people make mind maps?
3 Do you use mind maps?

2 Ahmet made a mind map to help him with a presentation. What is the topic?

3 Complete Ahmet's mind map with the words and phrases below.

1 football
2 Where?
3 magazines
4 at the weekend

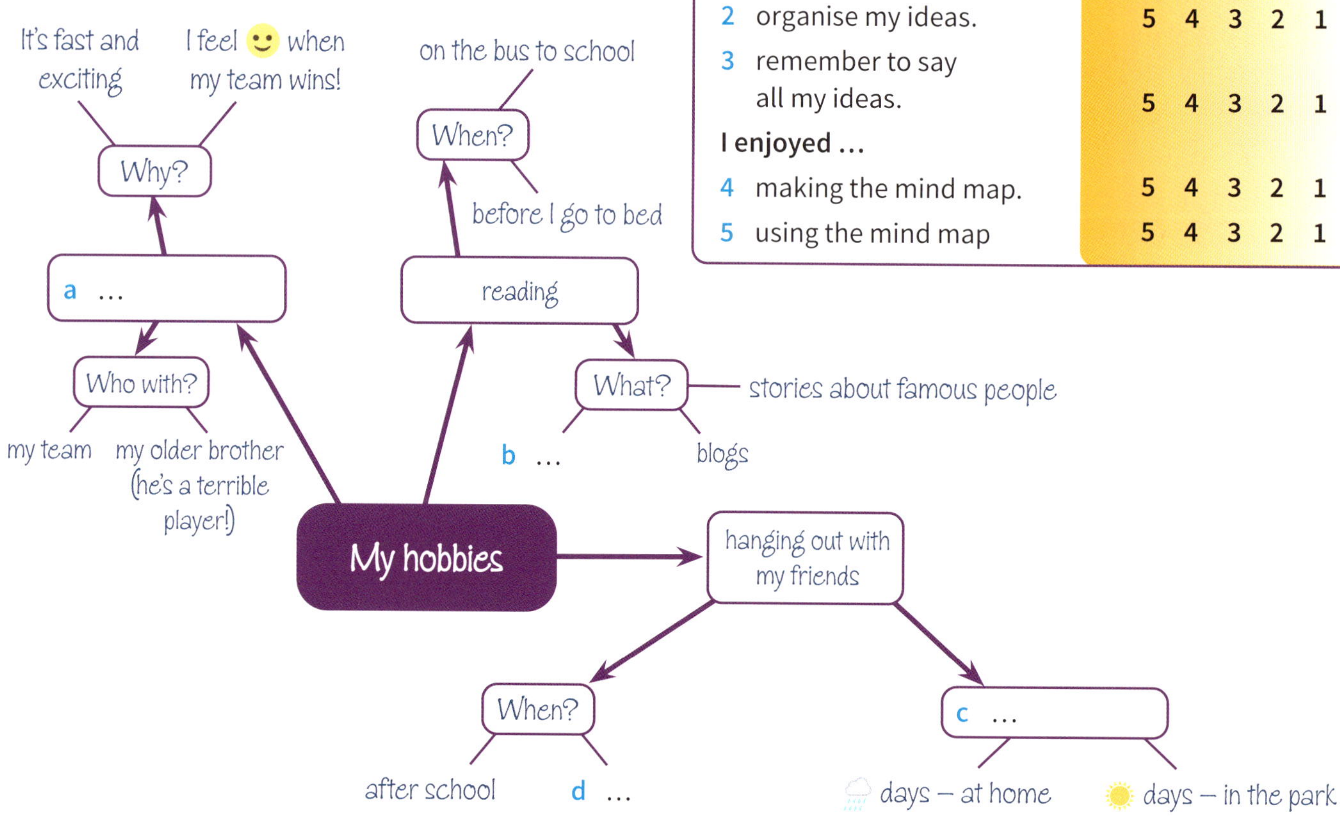

4 Make a mind map about your favourite animal. Follow the instructions.

1 Write the topic in the middle.
2 Add three main ideas about the topic.
3 Write one or two questions about each main idea.
4 Write notes about your answers to each question.

5 Use your mind map to talk to your partner about your favourite animal.

6 How do you feel? Compare and discuss your answers with a partner.

The mind map helped me ...	agree → disagree
1 think of ideas.	5 4 3 2 1
2 organise my ideas.	5 4 3 2 1
3 remember to say all my ideas.	5 4 3 2 1
I enjoyed ...	
4 making the mind map.	5 4 3 2 1
5 using the mind map	5 4 3 2 1

Search online for a digital mind mapping tool. Use it to brainstorm, to organise the ideas you might need and to plan. Share your findings with your classmates.

LEARN TO LEARN

LEARN TO ... IMPROVE YOUR WRITING

When you write something, ask your partner to check it. This improves your writing and your partner's writing.

1 Read the writing task and Oleg's story. Correct Oleg's mistakes to help him improve.

WRITING TASK

Write a story about a fun day you had in your town.

- Write between 50 and 70 words.
- Use words for places in town and personal possessions.
- Use the past simple.
- Describe people, places and things to make it interesting.
- Give your story a title.

Don't forget to use punctuation and check your spelling!

A nice day I had in town by Oleg

Last Saturday it [1]is was my birthday. My [2]parent ... gave me a skateboard. In the morning I went to the skate [3]parc ... to try it. In the afternoon, I met my friend Boris. We love fish, so we visited the aquarium and saw lots of fish. I didn't [4]took ... any photos because I [5]leaved ... my phone at home, but Boris took lots. In the evening I [6]have ... dinner with my family in a restaurant.

2 Which emojis in the checklist would Oleg choose?

Checklist for story writing task		
	Oleg	**My partner**
Did he/she ...		
1 write about the topic?	🙁 😐 🙂	🙁 😐 🙂
2 write between 50 and 70 words?	🙁 😐 🙂	🙁 😐 🙂
3 use words for places in town?	🙁 😐 🙂	🙁 😐 🙂
4 use words for possessions?	🙁 😐 🙂	🙁 😐 🙂
5 use the past simple?	🙁 😐 🙂	🙁 😐 🙂
6 make it interesting?	🙁 😐 🙂	🙁 😐 🙂
7 add a title?	🙁 😐 🙂	🙁 😐 🙂
8 use punctuation?	🙁 😐 🙂	🙁 😐 🙂
9 use correct spelling?	🙁 😐 🙂	🙁 😐 🙂

3 Work in pairs. Imagine your partner is Oleg. Use your answers in the checklist in Exercise 2 to tell him what you like and what he can improve.

You used words for places in a town. That was good!

Thanks!

You can improve your past simple. You made some mistakes.

OK. Thank you for your help.

4 Write your own story for the task in Exercise 1.

5 Give your partner your story. Choose the emojis in the checklist in Exercise 2 about your partner's story.

6 Use your answers in the checklist to tell your partner what you like and what they can improve.

After writing something, share it with your classmates. Invite them to make a short audio or video recording of their thoughts. Check their feedback and learn from it to improve your writing. Share your findings with your classmates.

LEARN TO LEARN

LEARN TO ... MAKE AN ACTION PLAN

An action plan can help you improve a little every day.

1 Read the texts and answer these questions.

Who ...

1 watches films? *Sasha*
2 reads blogs?
3 watches online videos?
4 reads books?
5 listens to songs?
6 chats with a friend?
7 uses an app?

I have an app on my phone with flashcards. I use it a lot and sometimes I watch films in English. I also love English pop music. I find the words of songs online, check their meaning, and sing in my bedroom!

I read fashion blogs in English, and lots of books too. Also, my best friend Anita and I sometimes chat in English. I don't usually watch films, because they're difficult, but I watch lots of videos online.

2 Choose three ways to practise English from Exercise 1. Tell your partner why you want to try them.

I chose 'read a blog'.

Me, too! Why did you choose that?

Because I love reading online.

3 Write the three things you chose in Exercise 2 and how often you will do them.

read a blog: twice a week

4 Use your answers to Exercise 3 to make an action plan.

Action plan							
	Monday	Tuesday	Wednesday	Thursday	Friday	Saturday	Sunday
read a blog	✓			✓			

5 Tell your partner about your action plan. Are there any things you can do together?

What are you going to do?

I'm going to watch a film in English once a week.

We can do that together! You can come to my house.

Search online for a graphic design tool to create a digital infographic. Use it to create an action plan and check how it helps you to improve. Share your findings with your classmates.

MEDIATION PRACTICE

DEVELOPING SUMMARISING SKILLS: UNDERSTANDING PERSPECTIVES

1 Look at the title and pictures in the text. What can you see? What can you remember about this text? Tell your partner.

A day in the life of …

This is Amir from the Bajau tribe in Borneo. His life is unusual. He lives with his family in a house – but it's in the water. Amir doesn't know his age or the date of his birthday. The Bajau tribe don't count days and hours; they use the movement of the sea to count time.

Every morning, Amir wakes up early, but he doesn't have breakfast. He and his father go out in their boat. They swim in the water to look for food for the day. Amir and the people in his tribe can see really well under water. Amir catches a fish for breakfast and his father catches an octopus for dinner.

After breakfast, Amir usually meets his friends. They don't go to school and they don't study subjects like English. The older Bajau people teach them how to make nets and build boats.

In the afternoons, Amir and his friends dive into the water from bridges and they play in the water, too. It's their favourite place!

In the evenings, Amir's mother and sisters cook the octopus and then the family has dinner together. It's always delicious!

2 **Student A:** Read the text and imagine you are Amir. Think about your everyday life and in your notebook, make notes about: your daily routine; what you enjoy/don't enjoy about your life; and what life is like for your parents.
Student B: Read and imagine you are Amir's parents. Think about your everyday life and in your notebook, make notes about: your daily routine; what you enjoy/don't enjoy about your life; and what life is like for your son.

3 Summarise your notes and compare with your partner. Use the prompts in the box.

Student A – Perspective 1	Student B - Perspective 2
Amir likes/doesn't like …	Amir's mother/father likes/ doesn't like …
Amir thinks his parents …	Amir's parents think that he …

4 Compare your life to Amir's. What's the same and what's different?

Sub-skill: Emotional Development

Understanding different perspectives is a strength not a weakness. Do you agree? Why / Why not?

5 Now think of another person who is the same age as you, e.g. a character from a book or a TV show or a real person. Think about their life and compare it to your own life. Summarise your ideas to your partner.

6 REFLECT Were you able understand a different perspective in a text?

DEVELOPING SUMMARISING SKILLS: WHAT'S THE GIST?

1 Look at the pictures in the fact files. What can you see? Tell your partner.

Animals with a difference

Part A

Snowflake

From 1964 until 2003, there was a special gorilla in Barcelona Zoo. His name was Snowflake, and he was born in Africa. Snowflake was a celebrity in the zoo. He wasn't the same as the other gorillas because he was white. He was the world's only white gorilla.

WEIGHT Up to 270 kg
HABITAT African forests and mountains
FOOD Fruit, leaves and plants
FACT Gorillas are the largest mammals to build nests. They make a new nest every night!

Part B

Nómade

In the 1990s, in Mozambique, southern Africa, a baby elephant was born without tusks. Her name was Nómade. Her 11 sisters were born without them, too. In the 1930s, there weren't many African elephants without tusks, only 1%. But, in some areas of Africa today, 98% of female elephants are born like this.

WEIGHT Up to 6,000 kg
HABITAT African savannah and forests
FOOD Grass, leaves, trees, fruit and plants
FACT Elephants use their feet to listen.

2 Work in groups of three.
Student A: Read Part A
Student B: Read Part B
Student C: Read Part C
In your notebook, make notes about:

The animal – What type of animal is it?
Location – Where is the animal from? / Where does it live now?
Unusual information – What makes this animal different?
Extra details – What other information can you find?

Part C

Artico

In 2004, a Bengal tiger called Artico was born in a wildlife centre in Alicante, Spain. Artico wasn't like his parents. He was white with no stripes, but his parents weren't. They were orange with black stripes. Today, there are only about 20 Bengal tigers without stripes in the world.

WEIGHT Up to 230 kg
HABITAT Forests and mountains in Southeast Asia
FOOD Deer, buffalo, antelopes and other animals
FACT There aren't two tigers with the same stripes!

3 Summarise your part to your group and answer any questions. Use the prompts in the box.

Summarising language	Questions / Responses
The text is about ...	What type of animal is it?
It's unusual because ...	What does it eat?
Here's an interesting fact, ...	Where does it live?
Did you know ... ?	Really? / That's interesting!

Sub-skill: Critical Thinking

Do you think it is better for some animals to be in a zoo? Why / Why not?

4 Now research another animal. Work with a new partner and summarise the information you have found. Use Exercise 2 as a guide. Ask questions and respond.

5 REFLECT Were you able to summarise the text to your partner?

MEDIATION PRACTICE

DEVELOPING SUMMARISING SKILLS: ROLL AND RETELL

1 Look at the photo. Can you remember what this text is about?

The Girl and the Golden Eagle

The 2016 film, *The Eagle Huntress*, tells the story of Aisholpan. When she was young, Aisholpan took care of her father's eagle but she really wanted to be an eagle hunter like her father. So she went to the high Altai Mountains with her father to find a baby eagle to train. It wasn't easy. The climb to the eagle nest was difficult and dangerous. But Aisholpan did it. She found her baby eagle!

Aisholpan's father became her trainer. But was Aisholpan strong enough to hunt with the huge bird in freezing temperatures? Yes, because she was determined to succeed.

In 2016, Aisholpan competed in the Golden Eagle Festival. She was the first Mongolian girl to enter the competition. There were 70 competitors. She was the youngest and the only girl. And guess what? Her eagle won. What an amazing achievement!

2 **Read the text. Work with a partner and retell the story of 'The Eagle Huntress' to each other. Follow the instructions below.**
Student A: Roll a dice. Ask your partner the question associated with the number on the dice.
Student B: Answer your partner's question. Then roll the dice and repeat the steps.

1 Who are the main characters?
2 Where does the story take place?
3 What is the story about / What is unusual in the story?
4 What happens at the beginning?
5 What happens in the middle?
6 What happens in the end?

Sub-skill: Communication

In communication, speaking is more important than listening – do you agree? Why / Why not?

3 Now think of another story that you both know, e.g. from a book, TV show or film. Roll the dice and retell the story together. Use Exercise 2 as a guide.

4 REFLECT Were you able to answer questions about the film?

DEVELOPING RELAYING SKILLS: COOPERATIVE READING

1 Look at the title in the text. Does your country have summer camps? Tell your partner.

Sub-skill: Collaboration

Can you think of five tips to help people collaborate well?

Part A

Tech Camp, Massachusetts

You'll be in a great university in the state, at the heart of technology! In just three weeks, you'll learn to build robots with our older students. They'll help you to develop useful skills like game and web design. You'll stay in an apartment on our beautiful campus and experience college life.

Part B

Languages for Life, Georgia

Learn a new language! Choose from Arabic, Chinese and lots more! You'll live and sleep in the language and culture. You won't speak English for a month! In your free time, why not visit the world's largest aquarium or one of Georgia's wonderful museums?

Part C

Advanced Soccer Skills, California

Los Angeles has a long history of sport – the Summer Olympics in 1932 and 1984 and in 2028 the Olympics will be here again! In just one week, our professional coaches will use your natural talent to teach you amazing new soccer skills. Sorry no beginners!

Part D

Theater School, New Jersey

New Jersey is home to one of the most successful performing arts centers in the USA. Develop your musical talents or choose from circus skills, magic, public speaking or acting! After two weeks here, you'll perform live on the last day.

2 Work in groups of four.

Student A: Read Part A **Student B:** Part B
Student C: Read Part C **Student D:** Part D

In your notebook, make notes about the following:

What are the key words and phrases in your paragraph?

What is the main idea in your paragraph?

Predict which members of your group would like to attend this camp.

3 Compare your notes with someone else in the class who is looking at the same part. Can you add any more details?

4 Next, go back to your group of four and take turns to relay (describe) your part to each other in your first language. Were your predictions correct?

5 REFLECT Were you able to relay information from your text to your group?

MEDIATION TASK

STUDENT A

PREPARE

1 Read the text. Copy the mind map into your notebook and complete it with information from the text.

Most Inspiring Women with Disability

FRANCESCA MARTINEZ is a comedian, writer, actor and campaigner. She was born in London in 1978. Her father is Spanish and her mother is half Swedish and half English. When she was 20 years old, she was the first female to win a special award for comedy at the Edinburgh Festival in Scotland. As a campaigner, she often speaks about austerity, climate change, racism, and disability rights at many major events. Francesca also regularly appears on television and supports charities, including *Global Angels,* a charity that helps to transform communities for the better. Francesca was born with cerebral palsy, a condition that makes it difficult to control muscles, but she prefers to describe herself as 'wobbly'.

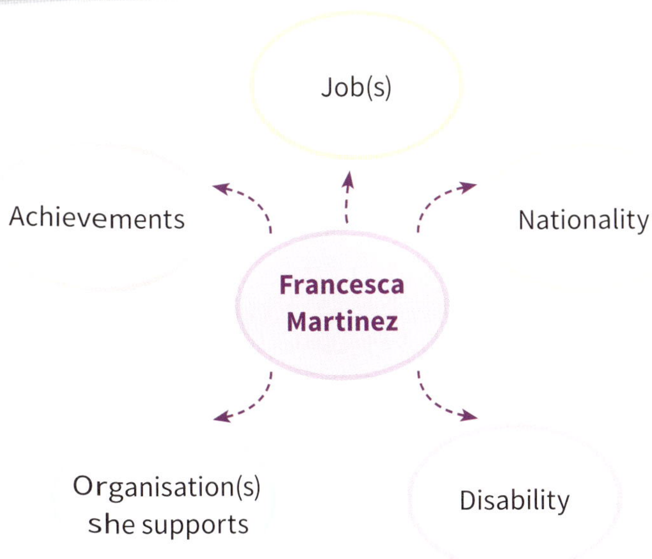

TASK

2 Tell Student B about Francesca Martinez. Use your notes from Exercise 1.

Francesca Martinez is a …. She's from ….
She's famous / successful because …

3 Listen to Student B and make a new mind map for Beatrice Vio.

4 Compare your information and answer the following questions:

- What are the similarities between the two people?

  Both Francesca and Beatrice are ….

- What are the differences between the two people?

  Beatrice …. but Francesca …

- What's the most interesting fact about each person?

  Beatrice I think the most interesting thing about Beatrice is …

Digital Extension

Go online and find another inspiring person. Find three interesting facts about the person and summarise the information for the class. Use the mind map to help you.

MEDIATION TASK

STUDENT B

PREPARE

1 Read the text. Copy the mind map into your notebook and complete it with information from the text.

Most Inspiring Women with Disability

BEATRICE VIO, also known as Bebe Vio, is a Paralympic wheelchair fencer from Italy. She was born in Venice in 1997. When she was 11 years old, she was very ill. Doctors saved her life, but not her arms or her legs. After only 100 days, she was able to go back to school. She was just 17 when she was the European champion. In 2015, she was the world champion and then in 2016, she was the Paralympic champion. Bebe Vio works with the organisation *art4sport*. They help children with disabilities do their favourite sport. Bebe is also very creative. She draws pictures and puts them on T-shirts and other clothes. They sell them to raise money to help the organisation.

TASK

2 Tell Student A about Beatrice Vio. Use your notes from Exercise 1.

Beatrice Vio is a …. She's from ….
She's famous / successful because …

3 Listen to Student A and make a new mind map for Francesca Martinez.

4 Compare your information and answer the following questions:

- What are the similarities between the two people?

  Both Francesca and Beatrice are ….

- What are the differences between the two people?

  Beatrice …. but Francesca …

- What's the most interesting fact about each person?

  Beatrice I think the most interesting thing about Beatrice is …

Digital Extension

Go online and find another inspiring person. Find three interesting facts about the person and summarise the information for the class. Use the mind map to help you.